Making Church
Accessible to All

Text copyright © BRF 2013
The author asserts the moral right
to be identified as the author of this work

Published by
The Bible Reading Fellowship
15 The Chambers, Vineyard
Abingdon OX14 3FE
United Kingdom
Tel: +44 (0)1865 319700
Email: enquiries@brf.org.uk
Website: www.brf.org.uk
BRF is a Registered Charity

ISBN 978 0 85746 157 5

First published 2013

10 9 8 7 6 5 4 3 2 1 0

Acknowledgments
Unless otherwise stated, scripture quotations are taken from the Holy Bible, New International
Version (Anglicised edition), copyright © 1979, 1984, 2011 by Biblica (formerly International
Bible Society). Used by permission of Hodder & Stoughton Publishers, an Hachette UK
company. All rights reserved. 'NIV' is a registered trademark of Biblica (formerly International
Bible Society). UK trademark number 1448790.

Scripture quotations taken from the HOLY BIBLE: EASY-TO-READ VERSION™ © 2006 by
World Bible Translation Center, Inc. are used by permission.

'All hail the Lamb' by Dave Bilbrough © 1987 Thankyou Music. *Adm. by worshiptogether.
com songs excl. UK & Europe, adm. by Kingswaysongs, a division of David C Cook
tym@kingsway.co.uk

The paper used in the production of this publication was supplied by mills that source their
raw materials from sustainably managed forests. Soy-based inks were used in its printing and
the laminate film is biodegradable.

A catalogue record for this book is available from the British Library

Printed and bound by CPI Group (UK) Ltd, Croydon, CR0 4YY

Making Church Accessible to All

Including disabled people in church life

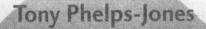

Tony Phelps-Jones

Other contributors:
**Gill Behenna, Jonathan Clark,
Ann Memmott, Kay Morgan-Gurr,
Mike Townsend, Tracy Williamson, Tim Wood**

Acknowledgments

Tony has written Chapters 1 to 8 of this book. Chapters 9 to 14 have been written by people with significant personal experience in the different disability fields covered. Each writer is introduced at the beginning of their chapter. Tony would like to thank each one of them for their invaluable contribution and for making this book possible.

Tony would also like to pay tribute to David and Madeleine Potter, who pioneered effective ministry among people with learning disabilities through the work of Prospects, and whose expertise and humility have inspired many others to become involved and transformed the lives of thousands of people with learning disabilities. Tony's own ministry developed out of working with and learning from David and Madeleine.

A special thank you to Gordon Temple, whose support and help in the final stages of preparation has been such an encouragement.

Contents

Foreword

When Maggie came up to receive Holy Communion for the first time, she refused to take the translucent round wafer of bread that was offered. Her parents were understandably distressed. We had been preparing for this day for some months. Maggie was living with severe learning disabilities, but she loved church and it seemed as if she had been looking forward to her first communion. She had certainly enjoyed being part of the preparation group I had run. But something went wrong on the day. Something was preventing Maggie from feeling included.

I think it was her big sister who quietly pointed out that Maggie probably didn't recognise that little round wafer as food. Why would you take such a thing and put it in your mouth? The following week we consecrated a small piece of 'real bread' for Maggie. She never looked back.

This little story illustrates two truths about this important book. First, our churches need to change and adapt and learn how to include people, especially those with learning disabilities or autism or hearing loss or mental health conditions, who are so often excluded elsewhere. Secondly, though, we have so much to learn from others, especially the excluded, the ignored and those on the margins. The Bible is full of examples of God speaking through unlikely people—or, should we say, the people we least expect. And God is always toppling the mighty from their thrones.

Maggie was saying something important to the whole church about the nature of eucharistic hospitality. She was teaching us. Therefore, when we become a church which is accessible to everyone, we will be open to hearing everyone's voice and we will be closer to becoming the church that God intends us to be. This book will help your church understand these issues of inclusion and accessibility. It also offers practical wisdom. Read it and the doors of your church will be opened.

Stephen Cottrell
Bishop of Chelmsford

Introduction

Visiting a windmill while on holiday in France, I learned the French word for chatterbox: *moulin à paroles*, literally, a 'word mill'. I embark on writing this book acutely aware of the risk of being simply a *moulin à paroles*, churning out words to be received only with polite interest or irritated boredom.

The words and language we use are crucial for communication, but both words and language evolve and change. Words we were happy to use ten years ago are now deemed out of place. Not only that, but our language is full of jargon in almost every sphere of life, not least the church.

A book that tackles disability and the church, looking for a happy and seamless blending of the two, is almost guaranteed to hit the jargon button and cause confusion. So please bear with me as I explain some of the words and phrases that will appear in its pages, in the hope that you will read on with understanding instead of stopping the *moulin à paroles* and putting the book back on the shelf.

Making church 'accessible'

Many words are understood differently depending on who's speaking, who's listening and where they are being spoken. The words 'saving' and 'redeeming', spoken by a clerk in a bank, would mean very different things if they were spoken by a minister in a church. Words such as 'service' and 'praise' are commonly used in everyday speech but have a particular meaning in church circles.

The *Concise Oxford English Dictionary* defines 'accessible' as 'able to be reached, entered, influenced or understood', and 'church' as 'a building for public worship or a body of Christians'. So an accessible church could be a building for public worship in which barriers to entry are removed so that anyone at all can get in, move around and make use of all the facilities.

Where 'church' refers to a group of people, the definition is harder. 'Accessible' in this case might mean that it is easy to make and build relationships and friendships there, or that visitors are easily accepted—much harder things to measure.

So what does 'inclusive' mean?

We could say that the word 'accessible' is to do with the building and 'inclusive' is to do with the people. Being accessible makes it possible for people to gain entry and join in. Being inclusive goes way beyond that, describing how we are as people—our attitude and approach to others, the warmth of welcome for new arrivals, the encouragement and support given so that people can get the most out of what church has to offer and can feel at home there.

So that gets us beyond the book and chapter titles! What about the word 'disability'? The most commonly recognised symbol representing disability is the wheelchair; it's visual and easy to understand. Many people's response to that idea is, 'Solve the wheelchair user's problems and you're there, or at least well on the way.' Statistics show, however, that only seven per cent of disabled people are wheelchair users. That still represents a large number of people, so meeting their needs is a good start, but it leaves much more to be done.

Another common misunderstanding is about the prevalence of disability in society. Many consider it to be a marginal issue affecting a small minority of people, but the fact is that there are ten million disabled people in the UK—one person in six. Among people over the age of 50, the proportion rises.

In addition, it is estimated that 95 per cent of people will experience a disabling condition at some point in their lives. This is no marginal issue that we may or may not come across. It is very much an 'us' rather than a 'them' matter, and should be seen as a mainstream issue. It needs to be brought into clear focus for attention and action so that the church of Christ becomes fully accessible and inclusive.

Think of it like this. One family in four is affected by disability. If a church is able to welcome, support, encourage and include the disabled family member, the impact on the whole family will be positive and lasting. The converse is likely to be equally true. Where a church is unprepared or copes badly with the arrival of a disabled person, not only the individual but the whole family could be alienated.

This book is in two parts. The first part looks at issues to weigh up and think about. The second is an essentially practical approach, tackling seven areas of disability, taking the theory of Part 1 and examining how to put it into practice.

Much of what is contained in this book could be described as common sense. But it's only common sense when you know what the issues are, and that's what you can expect to discover as you read on. You will also gain wisdom and insight from the people who have contributed to the book. Each one brings his or her knowledge and experience to bear in ways that will inform and inspire you.

My prayer is that you will enjoy the journey through these pages and respond to the challenges they contain, for there are many. By God's grace, may we see increasing numbers of churches where disabled people are welcomed, included, encouraged and strengthened, and where their presence and gifts in the congregation bless others and make for a church that is rich in love—in short, a church that is better for everyone.

Part 1

WELCOME!

Chapter 1
Inclusive people

The steward pushed the church door shut and hit the panic button. The Duty Deacon came running. 'What's wrong? What's wrong?' he shouted.

The steward explained that there was a man outside who wanted to come into the service.

'A man? That's wonderful!' said the DD.

'Well, not really,' said the steward. 'You see, he's in a wheelchair!'

'Oh dear,' replied the DD. 'How will we get him up the steps? And what about the fixed pews? I'll go and ask the pastor.'

The Bible gives a very clear and positive picture of what church should be like. In 1 Corinthians 12, the apostle Paul likens the church to a body with many parts, all different but all essential and valued. As we think about welcoming people into the building we call church, we start by recognising that only Christ, through grace, can bring people into the body of Christ, the people we call church. 'For we were all baptised by one Spirit so as to form one body—whether Jews or Gentiles, slave or free—and we were all given the one Spirit to drink' (1 Corinthians 12:13).

Paul expands on this theme of grace in Ephesians 2. Motivated by love, God has demonstrated what is humanly impossible—salvation by grace: 'But because of his great love for us, God, who is rich in mercy, made us alive with Christ even when we were dead in transgressions—it is by grace you have been saved' (Ephesians 2:4–5). People who believe and trust in Christ have, by the grace of God, been taken from death to life. Once saved by grace and therefore made part of the body of Christ, people should not fall into the trap of looking around and comparing themselves with others, concluding perhaps that they don't fit or don't belong. It is not a matter of whether or not we are good enough or worthy of God's favour; we are not! But through God's grace we are transformed and welcome in his presence.

Paul comments on this in his comparison of the church with a human body:

Now if the foot should say, 'Because I am not a hand, I do not belong to the body,' it would not for that reason stop being part of the body. And if the ear should say, 'Because I am not an eye, I do not belong to the body,' it would not for that reason stop being part of the body.
(1 CORINTHIANS 12:15–16)

How we are made and how we fit in is part of God's amazing plan for his people and his church. Each one of us is unique, yet we each have a place to take alongside others.

Paul continues to press the argument by saying that no one may judge another to be unnecessary. As every part of the body is essential, so is every person in the membership of a church: 'The eye cannot say to the hand, "I don't need you!" And the head cannot say to the feet, "I don't need you!" On the contrary, those parts of the body that seem to be weaker are indispensable' (vv. 21–22).

Verse 22 is a very powerful and intriguing statement. It refers to people who 'seem to be weaker'. Disability does not equate to weakness. Sure, there may be some things a disabled person can't do, but equally there may be things they excel in. There is a danger that we may see only the person's disability and fail to see their abilities, strengths and gifts. The weakness referred to in verse 22 is an *apparent* weakness—our perception of their weakness—based perhaps on comparisons with ourselves or others. We are not to judge like that. Such judgment can lead to discrimination and is out of place in the Christian church.

Indeed, there is much for those who are considered strong to learn from the weak, and for the rich to learn from the poor.

Brothers and sisters, think of what you were when you were called. Not many of you were wise by human standards; not many were influential; not many were of noble birth. But God chose the foolish things of the world to shame the wise; God chose the weak things of the world to shame the strong. God chose the lowly things of this world and the despised things—and the things that are not—to nullify the things that are, so that no one may boast before him.
(1 CORINTHIANS 1:26–29)

'Those parts that seem to be weaker' describes, of course, a host of people in different life circumstances, but certainly would include some people with disabilities. The surprising conclusion from this analysis of scripture is that where a church recognises and addresses the needs of people with disabilities, investing time, effort and resources into making church a better place for them, the church will become a stronger, more united, loving church—a better place for everyone.

And it works! I asked church leaders to share their stories.

Kerith Centre, Bracknell

Simon Benham, senior pastor at Kerith Community Church, Bracknell, writes:

Over the last 25 years, Kerith has been on a journey of becoming more and more accessible to people with disabilities. It started with us providing signing for the deaf community on a Sunday, but now includes running a group for adults with learning disabilities, providing respite care, support groups, advocacy and Sunday buddies for families with children with special needs, and modifying our building to include better facilities for people with physical disabilities.

This journey has transformed us as a church. Being more aware of people with disabilities has helped us to recognise that we all have areas where we struggle and where we need to make allowances for one another. We have become more real about our own struggles, more open about our own weaknesses and more compassionate about reaching out to people who are different to us.

Riverside Church, Exeter

Aran Richardson is senior pastor at Riverside Church, Exeter, and has a son with learning disabilities. He writes:

Over the last few years we have seen a change in the programmes that the church offers. A sensory room has been installed adjacent to the youth and children's facilities. This space is now accessed by local school groups as part of their SENCO requirements as well as a weekly Parent and Toddler support group for parents of children with special needs.

Other programmes are delivered specifically with inclusion in mind. We aim to give all people the opportunity to engage with all our service programmes.

For example, a girl with partial sight wanted to take part in a day out cycling along the river path. Individually, this was beyond her abilities, but aboard a tandem she was able to be part of everything that happened on the day. And the arrival of a boy with autism at our Friday night youth project has led to his peer group picking up a few simple Makaton signs in order to engage with him. They are learning to accommodate him, but also to accept him as part of the group in a practical (rather than idealistic) way. This attitude holds true across the church.

A short while back, one of the young people who has autism displayed a desire to be part of the worship band. Although they didn't have the necessary ability to play an instrument, the worship leader open-tuned a guitar to the appropriate key and allowed the young person to be part of the worship set that evening. The young person strummed away merrily, and it really was a memorable evening and a great example of how inclusive we can be if we put our hearts and minds into it.

We're far from perfect, and there are many areas in which we could improve. Ultimately, Riverside exists to connect people with God and to build a community of believers, and we will continue to work towards an environment that allows that to happen for everyone.

Go and do likewise

'What must I do to inherit eternal life?' (Luke 10:25). The question opened a dialogue between the legal expert and Jesus. The man knew the law and summarised the commandments exactly as Jesus himself does in Matthew 22:37–39: 'Love the Lord your God with all your heart and with all your soul and with all your strength and with all your mind,' and 'Love your neighbour as yourself.' But it was not enough for him that Jesus commended his answer. He wanted to know what was meant by 'neighbour'.

As Jesus told the story of the good Samaritan, his listeners would have been shocked—not by the violent action of the robbers (that was to be expected) but by the callous behaviour of the priest and the Levite, and the intervention of the Samaritan. The hated foreigner was the one who stopped and got his hands dirty, shaming those whose calling should have prompted them to help. It's a simple enough message: keep your eyes open for people in need of help, and get stuck in.

Some church members may need extra help and support in order to be included and effective, and that's fine. It's part of the mutual respect and honour with which we should treat each other. It has positive outcomes: it promotes the concern Christians should have for one another and it minimises the risk of divisions. As we invest our time and effort in promoting equality and harmony, we will have less time and inclination to enter into squabbles and arguments over matters of little consequence.

Disabled people and their families often need help and support, some more than others. Having spotted a need, it's a matter of sensitively asking the question, 'Is there anything I can do to help?' Provided that the offer is genuine and not patronising, people will not mind being asked, and it may start off a fruitful conversation and relationship.

Obedience to Jesus' command to 'go and do likewise' may lead us to give practical, emotional or spiritual support to a disabled person. That's a great start, and to be commended. But what many people discover is that, while the initial motivation and action put them in the role of giver, it's not long before they find themselves on the receiving end. As the relationship develops, the helper is blessed by the person they are helping.

Judy's story

Having been involved with *La Ciudad Feliz* ('the Happy City') project in Ecuador since the 1980s, I have been privileged to meet many of the children helped by safe housing and education.

One of these children was Paulo, an underweight, diminutive child of seven, found sleeping in the bus station of Ambato, a major city. Paulo had no hope of bettering himself, whether physically, because he begged and 'borrowed' to survive, educationally, because he had a mental age of three, or spiritually, because no one was there to tell him that God even existed, let alone loved and cared for him. Paulo wasn't an attractive boy. He had uncorrected crossed eyes and was able to relate only to dogs, ignoring any attempt by adults to engage verbally or in sign language. Dogs somehow knew what Paulo needed, so a wagging tail or lick of the cheek brought a beatific smile to his weathered face, showing broken and rotten teeth but a twinkle in his eyes and dimples in his cheeks.

The couple who lead the family at the Happy City, Ramiro and Jenny Vega, could see the possibilities in Paulo, and I met Paulo when I went to help build bedrooms there. We incorporated prayer times, Bible study, singing and playing with the 17 or more children who lived there and those who ran through the fields to arrive for play time. Paulo always stood apart, unable to relate well with a group. I tried, by moving near him and getting him used to my presence, to involve him gradually in the fun. Slowly, slowly…

During that visit, I received news that a beloved uncle had died. Several times, I took myself away to think of him and pray for the family I couldn't join in their grief. At one of those times, I suddenly became aware of a little shadow accompanying me. It was Paulo. Somehow he was in tune with my sadness and *he* came alongside *me*, intuitively offering me the loving support I needed. Without words or touch, he was just *there*.

JUDY DIVALL, HAMPSHIRE

The last word

Lesley Biffen speaks about her faith in Christ and her passion for people with additional needs to be made welcome in church. She has learning disabilities and is supported by Prospects:

Jesus is the light and the life of everything.

Chapter 2
Inclusive God

The pastor was a resourceful man and quickly directed two of his elders to go across the road to the railway station, where he had noticed a folding ramp leaning against a wall, while a third elder moved the church flowers so that the wheelchair could be put at the front of the congregation.

Just as the elders were about to leave the building, the steward caught them, a shocked expression on his face. 'But he also has Down's Syndrome!' That stopped them in their tracks—but they knew what to do in times of panic. 'I'll go and get the pastor,' said the senior elder.

In God's image

At the start of the footpath leading up from the west towards Pen y Fan, the highest peak in the Brecon Beacons, there's a National Park noticeboard explaining what you can expect as you explore the mountains. It names 'spiritual refreshment' as one of the three expectations. How interesting that the National Park authority recognises that being surrounded by the beauty and majesty of creation will result in spiritual refreshment.

At the beginning of Genesis, God says, 'Let there be light,' and the amazing work of creation begins. Water, land, plants, trees, sun, moon, stars, fish, birds, animals and people—a breathtaking array of diversity reflects the beauty and glory of God himself.

As Christians, we know why people would be refreshed by creation: it's the result of humans being made in the image of God. Genesis 1:26–27 says:

Then God said, 'Let us make mankind in our image, in our likeness, so that they may rule over the fish in the sea and the birds in the air, over the livestock and all the wild animals, and over all the creatures that move along the ground.' So God created mankind in his own image, in the image of God he created them; male and female he created them.

The way we are made gives us the capacity to appreciate created beauty and to be creative ourselves. Being made in God's image means that we can love, build deep and long-lasting relationships, and experience powerful emotions. We can show compassion and we can use logic and reason. When God finished creating, he took a look at everything he'd made and concluded that 'it was very good' (v. 31).

Any encounter with creation has the capacity to leave people amazed, inspired, thankful, awestruck or full of praise. Creation speaks constantly about the Creator. Psalm 19:1–4 says:

The heavens declare the glory of God; the skies proclaim the work of his hands. Day after day they pour forth speech; night after night they reveal knowledge. They have no speech, they use no words; no sound is heard from them. Yet their voice goes out into all the earth, their words to the ends of the world.

Day after day, night after night, the glory of God is being communicated, but do people notice? Scripture says that people have no excuse for not knowing about God, because his divine nature and eternal power have been openly displayed for all to see: 'For since the creation of the world God's invisible qualities—his eternal power and divine nature—have been clearly seen, being understood from what has been made, so that people are without excuse' (Romans 1:20). Standing by the sea and watching waves break over the rocks, seeing the rapids or waterfalls on a river, or walking through a wood with the wind roaring through the trees all leave a deep impression. The stillness of a mountain lake reflecting perfectly the peaks beyond, a red kite riding the thermals above in lazy circles, or the perfectly formed petals of a rose in bloom can all touch a person deeply, triggering a desire to know the Creator as well as to enjoy his handiwork.

A young man arrived at church, entering into worship with a wholeheartedness and lack of inhibition that caught the leader's attention. The man had never been to church before. Why was he there? Well, on holiday in South Africa, he'd climbed a tree and, as he sat there watching the sunset, God spoke to him. He was converted and transformed in that moment and, ten years on, is worshipping and serving God wholeheartedly.

The spectacular variety of creation never ceases to amaze me. There are so many species of plants, animals and birds, with more being discovered every year. There are more colours than can be described by human language. The fullness and generosity in creation reflect the generosity of God and his desire that the created order should be richly varied, and, as part of that richness, that people should enjoy life to the full. In John 10:10 (ERV), Jesus says, 'I came to give life—life that is full and good.' God's love for all that he has created is clearly expressed in Psalm 145:8–10: 'The Lord is gracious and compassionate, slow to anger and rich in love. The Lord is good to all; he has compassion on all he has made. All your works praise you, Lord; your faithful people extol you.'

Humans occupy a unique role in creation, having been given dominion over it and responsibility to care for it: 'God blessed them and said to them, "Be fruitful and increase in number; fill the earth and subdue it. Rule over the fish in the sea and the birds in the sky and over every living creature that moves on the ground"' (Genesis 1:28).

God's love for all people is expressed nowhere more clearly than in John 3:16: 'For God so loved the world that he gave his one and only Son, that whoever believes in him shall not perish but have eternal life.' 'Whoever believes...' No exceptions!

An awareness of God's love changes people, as Mary's story shows.

Just the way you are

Mary came by train. She'd travelled alone and it had been a very difficult journey. By the time she arrived, she was so upset that all she really wanted was to be back home. But the welcome encouraged her to stay, and that evening I taught a song beginning with the words, 'God loves you just the way you are, and he knows everything about you.' Mary could not accept that; it simply could not be true. She knew what her past contained, and she was certain that, if God really did know, he would not love her.

During the following day, team members chatted with her and, by the evening, she was persuaded. Not only did she lead us in singing verse 2 of the song, 'God loves me just the way I am', but her whole outlook on life had changed. Her face was now relaxed and smiling, her faith in a God of love renewed.

What Mary discovered was that God's love for people doesn't depend on how they behave, on how they have led their lives. Having made human beings in his image, God values and loves everyone so much that Jesus died on the cross for them. God's love is an amazing, compassionate love. It is a love that excludes nobody and discriminates against nobody— an inclusive love. This love, when expressed and understood, changes people's view of both God and themselves.

God has always been, and always will be. He has no beginning and no end; he is eternal and infinite. From our limited human perspective, this is difficult to comprehend. And God has never existed in isolation. Even when there was nothing else, there was the triune God, the Three-in-One: Father, Son and Holy Spirit.

The completeness of God in the Trinity is key when we are considering the nature of people in comparison with the nature of God. Genesis 1:1–2 and John 1:1 clearly link together Father, Son and Spirit at the point of creation: 'In the beginning God created the heavens and the earth. Now the earth was formless and empty, darkness was over the surface of the deep, and the Spirit of God was hovering over the waters'; 'In the beginning was the Word, and the Word was with God, and the Word was God.'

Luke 3:21–22 records the baptism of Jesus, when all three members of the Trinity made a public appearance:

When all the people were being baptised, Jesus was baptised too. And as he was praying, heaven was opened and the Holy Spirit descended on him in bodily form like a dove. And a voice came from heaven: 'You are my Son, whom I love; with you I am well pleased.'

Jesus emphasised to the disciples that they need look no further to discover the Father: 'I and the Father are one' (John 10:30) and 'Anyone who has seen me has seen the Father' (14:9). The writer to the Hebrews picks up this theme: 'The

Son is the radiance of God's glory and the exact representation of his being, sustaining all things by his powerful word' (Hebrews 1:3). The inclusive nature of God is demonstrated in the Trinity. They were together even from before the word 'Go'.

Genesis 1 concludes with verse 31: 'God saw all that he had made, and it was very good.' Everything that God had made was good, but something was missing. In Genesis 2:18 we read that God said, 'It is not good for the man to be alone. I will make a helper suitable for him.' In making people in his image, God made them to live in relationship with each other. God knew that human life would be incomplete without the contribution that others could bring.

That's why church and other forms of community engagement are so important as ingredients of normal life— and this is the link into the subject of disability. It is not just that disabled people need others, although you might argue that they do, but that all of us need the company and contribution of others if we are to enjoy the 'life to the full' that Jesus offers (John 10:10).

Some people with disabilities find themselves quite isolated. They may live alone, remote from family members or even rejected by them; they may be unable to get out easily, perhaps having lots of spare time and not much to fill it with. Please don't misunderstand me here: this is not a generalisation about disabled people. Many lead a full life, have dynamic relationships and are regularly in the company of family and friends. Many are involved in work or community activities in a leadership capacity.

For those who crave company and long for an extra dimension to life, though, God has provided other people—people like you and me. And God has provided the church, a gathering of people who share his values and long to see his kingdom made real on earth. For Christians, that may mean getting alongside people who live with difficult circumstances or have taken some serious knocks, and giving them encouragement, support, time and love so that they too can share 'life to the full'.

> *High king of heaven, thou heaven's bright sun,*
> *O grant me its joys after victory is won;*
> *Great heart of my own heart, whatever befall,*
> *Still be thou my vision, O ruler of all.*

Once we belong to the Father's family, we become sons and daughters of God. This last verse of the hymn 'Be thou my vision' lifts our eyes to the king of heaven, the ruler of all. If he is the king, then we, as his sons and daughters, are princes and princesses. Using this kind of graphic language to explain our status in God's kingdom can help people who may have been bombarded with negative messages about themselves. We can encourage them to agree with the psalmist that they are 'fearfully and wonderfully made' (Psalm 139:14) and help them to see that God's love for them was so great that Jesus died to win their forgiveness and salvation.

Chosen and loved

As people come to terms with this new and perhaps radical understanding of how God sees them, they may wonder about the purpose of it all. Amazed to be loved by God, astonished to be forgiven and set free from sin, thrilled to assume the status of royalty in God's kingdom, they may ask, 'But to what end?'

The answer lies in Ephesians 2:10: 'For we are God's handiwork, created in Christ Jesus to do good works, which

God prepared in advance for us to do.' In short, God has work for each one of us to do. It's something that God has been thinking about for some time, and it will bear fruit. It will not be the kind of task that leaves us scratching our heads. Because we are God's own handiwork, he will equip us fully for whatever task he calls us to. As we then, in faith, get on with it and achieve good results, God gets the glory. We are simply being obedient.

Some of the work to which God calls us may require us to make a stand against prejudice, discrimination or misunderstanding. Jesus was no stranger to such things, as the story of the man born blind illustrates (John 9). A commonly held belief in Jesus' time, and still in the present day in some countries and cultures, was that disability or disease was the result of sin. Therefore, the disciples ask, 'Who sinned, this man or his parents, that he was born blind?' (v. 2). Jesus makes it quite clear that they are on the wrong track, asking the wrong question.

As the story unfolds, the man's sight is restored, he and his parents are questioned, and he gradually gains confidence in his references to Jesus. By the end of the story he has become a worshipper (v. 38).

Jesus' whole lifestyle was an inclusive one. He often connected with people in a way that others in his position would not. On the way down from the mountain where he had been teaching the people about the kingdom of God, Jesus' path was crossed by a man with leprosy. It was unheard of for a rabbi to touch a person with leprosy, but Jesus broke the taboo and set him free: '[The man said], "Lord, if you are willing, you can make me clean." Jesus reached out his hand and touched the man. "I am willing," he said. "Be clean!" Immediately he was cleansed of his leprosy' (Matthew 8:2–3).

On another occasion, passing through Samaria, he met a woman at a well near Sychar. Jesus struck up a conversation with her, despite the cultural barriers that separated them and should have inhibited any contact.

The Samaritan woman said to him, 'You are a Jew and I am a Samaritan woman. How can you ask me for a drink?' (For Jews do not associate with Samaritans.) Jesus answered her, 'If you knew the gift of God and who it is that asks you for a drink, you would have asked him and he would have given you living water.' (JOHN 4:9–10)

Their conversation led to Jesus spending two days in Sychar, with many townspeople becoming believers as a result.

Hearing that Jesus was passing, blind Bartimaeus started shouting out and caught Jesus' attention. Jesus called him over and questioned him. '"What do you want me to do for you?" Jesus asked him. The blind man said, "Rabbi, I want to see." "Go," said Jesus, "your faith has healed you." Immediately he received his sight and followed Jesus along the road' (Mark 10:51–52).

Jesus' meeting with the unpopular Zacchaeus was greeted by discontented mutterings from the crowd. However, there were popular results as cheated people had their money restored: 'Zacchaeus stood up and said to the Lord, "Look, Lord! Here and now I give half of my possessions to the poor, and if I have cheated anybody out of anything, I will pay back four times the amount"' (Luke 19:8).

Through these unexpected encounters, Jesus brought blessing to the individual involved and often to others as well. Jesus made himself accessible to people, including them in his time, his ministry and his life. It's a pattern that we, as individuals and churches, will do well to emulate.

The last word

My favourite song is 'Jesus, be the centre'. For me, that says everything about Jesus.

LESLEY BIFFEN

Chapter 3
Inclusive thinking

His name was Michael. Dorothy discovered that. She had a job as a support worker in a community house for people with learning disabilities near the church, so she was delegated to sit beside the new arrival. His speech was a little indistinct but she persevered and managed a short conversation with him. He seemed to enjoy the service and came back the following week with a friend from the same house. James was much chattier and, by the time the service began, he'd introduced himself to everybody, surprising some of the ladies with a hug.

It was during the sermon that things began to go wrong. The pastor throws out lots of rhetorical questions as he preaches; we're used to that. But we're not used to people answering them! James reckoned he knew the answers to some of the questions and wasn't afraid to call them out. Each time, James and the pastor had a conversation about it, with the result that the sermon lasted 20 minutes longer than usual. That evening the pastor called the elders and deacons to an emergency meeting at his home.

I met Martin, a wheelchair user, at Spring Harvest. Happily married and in a position of responsibility at church, he was pleased to see how much was being done to make the event accessible and inclusive. He was grateful for the way his own church leaders recognised his strengths and gifts, supporting him so that he was able to serve effectively. Reflecting on other experiences, however, he made this observation: 'My biggest disability is other people's attitudes towards me.'

A dead dog

'What is your servant, that you should notice a dead dog like me?' (2 Samuel 9:8).

Mephibosheth was disabled. He'd been dropped by his nurse at the age of five as they fled the house, on hearing that Jonathan and Saul, his father and grandfather, had been killed in battle. In the ensuing power struggle for sovereignty over Israel, David, already king of Judah, gradually gained the upper hand over the house of Saul. Surviving members of Saul's family went into hiding and Mephibosheth was living in obscurity in Lo Debar.

Why did David call for Mephibosheth? 2 Samuel 9:7 gives us David's answer: 'I will surely show you kindness for the sake of your father Jonathan. I will restore to you all the land that belonged to your grandfather Saul, and you will always eat at my table.' His throne now secure over both Israel and Judah, David remembered his close friendship with Jonathan and recalled an occasion when he had made a promise to show kindness to Jonathan's family. Now, years later, he takes the opportunity to do just that and show kindness to Mephibosheth, Jonathan's son.

David's action had a profound impact on Mephibosheth's life.

- It restored family land to him. In Lo Debar, Mephibosheth had been dependent on Makir for a home, but now he had family land, a home and hope for the future.
- It met his financial needs. In addition to land, he was given Ziba's family to work the land and make it fruitful. His children would have a family business to provide for them.
- It restored his status. He had fled in fear, the grandson of a dead king, and vulnerable. David now called him to live in

Jerusalem and eat daily at the king's table, a privilege shared with the royal princes. He was being treated as if he were the king's son.

Many people with disabilities have suffered at the hands of others, finding themselves on the receiving end of abuse, discrimination or thoughtlessness. It can leave them feeling angry, rejected, isolated or lacking self-esteem.

David's response to Mephibosheth was deliberate and thought through. He had committed himself to take action, motivated by love. David's attitude towards Mephibosheth was publicly displayed in the way he honoured him, showed him generosity and drew him into a personal relationship as part not only of the king's court but also of his family around the table.

What motivates our response to disabled people? They are people loved by God, loved and valued by him every bit as much as I am and you are. As recipients ourselves of the grace and love of God, we seek to share his love without boundaries.

One passage of scripture that seems particularly relevant in this respect is Jesus' account of the sheep and goats in Matthew 25. The surprised reaction of those selected for commendation by the Lord for giving him help in his hour of need is, 'When did we see you a stranger and invite you in, or needing clothes and clothe you? When did we see you ill or in prison and go to visit you?' (Matthew 25:38–39). And the reply to their question is, 'Truly I tell you, whatever you did for one of the least of these brothers and sisters of mine, you did for me' (v. 40).

Acts of kindness to a person in need are the currency of Christian love, and will sow blessings into the lives of both the recipient of the kindness and the person who gives it.

Models of disability

The response of society to people with disabilities has changed over time. Advances in medicine have enabled better treatment and support, and legislation has been passed to protect people's rights. Several 'models' of disability have been developed and accepted as valid viewpoints, each addressing the issues from a different perspective.

The medical model

Are people with disabilities to be seen as needing a cure, help or care? That's where the medical model begins.

The medical model is the default position in a society where people go to the doctor to get their problems sorted. There's nothing wrong with that principle. We need medical expertise and hospitals. We need the interventions that can minimise pain, discomfort and health risks while maximising mobility and quality of life. The problem with the medical model, though, is that people can become defined by their disability rather than their personality. They become something to be 'fixed' or someone to be cared for. It can leave disabled people feeling that they've lost control of their lives, that others make the decisions for them. Dignity and independence are eroded.

The social model

This model asserts that what hinders or dis-ables people is not their limited physical or mental abilities but, rather, the failure of society to adapt or modify so that the everyday provisions of life are accessible and convenient for everybody. This means investment in the built environment and in the way we do things. It means giving disabled people not only a say in but also control over any support or care that they need to live a fulfilling life. The goal is independence.

The Disability Discrimination Act (1995) and the later Equality Act (2010) addressed some of these issues, but there is a danger that, as the rights of disabled people are championed, the issue can become a battle of rights in which the voice of reason and common sense gets lost—perhaps making non-disabled people wary of getting involved with disabled people.

The relational model

As we saw in Chapter 2, human beings are created to live in relationship with others rather than in isolation. It is through relationships that our character and values develop. In the relational model, we work together to make the best of any circumstances in a spirit of cooperation and mutual respect. We recognise that we are all dependent on others for elements of our daily life and needs, so a key word in this model is 'interdependency'. Everyone has something to contribute, from which others can benefit. This sits comfortably with the New Testament understanding of church and the indispensability of every person.

Each of the models we've considered can help our thought process, but the relational model draws us back to God as we consider God's view of people and their potential.

Jars of clay

'The god of this age has blinded the minds of unbelievers,' says Paul to the Corinthians, 'so that they cannot see the light of the gospel that displays the glory of Christ... For God... made his light shine in our hearts to give us the light of the knowledge of God's glory... But we have this treasure in jars of clay to show that this all-surpassing power is from God and not from us' (2 Corinthians 4:4, 6–7).

These verses are a real leveller. Whoever we are as Christians,

God has put his light in us, evidence of the glory of God at work in us and planted in us by the Holy Spirit. The wonder is that the glory of God can be shared with such rough clay pots as we are.

God's intention is for that light of Christ to shine out from us. As we seek and discover openness to God, more of the light of Christ can shine out. Disabled people are fully included in this picture and, through faith in Christ, can display God's glory.

Paul goes on in 2 Corinthians 4:8–10 to describe how his faith sustains him: 'We are hard pressed on every side, but not crushed; perplexed, but not in despair; persecuted, but not abandoned; struck down, but not destroyed. We always carry around in our body the death of Jesus, so that the life of Jesus may also be revealed in our body.' Many people with disabilities testify to the way the challenges they face have focused their faith and dependency on God and not only sustained them but equipped them to share their faith and strengthen others.

Full potential

I praise you because I am fearfully and wonderfully made; your works are wonderful, I know that full well. My frame was not hidden from you when I was made in the secret place, when I was woven together in the depths of the earth. Your eyes saw my unformed body; all the days ordained for me were written in your book before one of them came to be. (PSALM 139:14–16)

Psalm 139:14 reminds us that whoever we are, we are fearfully and wonderfully made, and that God knew us from conception and has watched over us ever since. What's more (v. 16), he has our future in his hands and has plans for us.

He has brought us through situations and experiences that have given us skills and wisdom to equip us to serve him in the future. We all have enormous potential, and God sees us not only as we are now but as we will be by his grace. People with disabilities can look forward to a future where they will be not only recipients of God's grace but also channels of his grace to others.

Sarah's story

Sarah Redgrove is quite open about having a learning disability and the things she found difficult as a result.

I don't mind people knowing that I struggled with church because of my learning disability. I just couldn't understand what people were talking about in church. Then I started going to a Prospects Ministry Group. They helped me to learn about Jesus, how he died for us and about forgiving everybody.

A fuller version of Sarah's story can be found in Chapter 8: 'Including people with learning disabilities'.

The last word

It is important for people with needs to know about Jesus. They have a right to know the truth about Jesus.
LESLEY BIFFEN

Chapter 4
Inclusive ministry

Two women arrived very early for the service, asking lots of questions. The Duty Deacon thought they might be mystery worshippers and brought them coffee and chocolate biscuits from the deacons' special reserve. One lady was deaf and the other said she was her interpreter.

They sat near the front, the deaf woman watching the interpreter intently. She wasn't the only one: most of the congregation were fascinated, with few paying attention to the pastor. During the sermon he became quite distracted himself, and his sermon lasted half its normal length. However, most people said they'd followed it more easily than usual, so they're hoping the ladies will come back.

Few churches are as radical and generous as the church described in Acts 2:42–47:

They devoted themselves to the apostles' teaching and to fellowship, to the breaking of bread and to prayer. Everyone was filled with awe at the many wonders and signs performed by the apostles. All the believers were together and had everything in common. They sold property and possessions to give to anyone who had need. Every day they continued to meet together in the temple courts. They broke bread in their homes and ate together with glad and sincere hearts, praising God and enjoying the favour of all the people. And the Lord added to their number daily those who were being saved.

The way these early disciples lived, related to each other and worshipped was enormously attractive, their numbers increasing daily. The Holy Spirit was at work in them and through them, and their newfound behaviour and lifestyle were enviable and infectious. Economic barriers were broken down as wealth and goods were shared (v. 45). Social barriers were overcome as people ate together (v. 46).

There was a strong commitment to learning the way of Christ ('They devoted themselves to the apostles' teaching'), creating a common and uniting desire to live with honesty and integrity, recognising the equal value of each person before God. Rich and poor people were equally welcome, as were both Jew and Gentile. No one was kept out. Prayer was also a key component of their community, emphasising the importance of the spiritual aspect of a person's life rather than their financial wealth, education or social standing.

Inclusivity—a new word?

Conductivity is a measure of how well a material allows electricity to pass through it. Copper has a very high conductivity, so a copper cable or bar will have low resistance to the flow of electric current through it. Plastic, ceramics and many other non-metallic materials have a very low conductivity. They resist the flow of electricity and therefore make good insulators, forming a barrier that the electric current cannot pass through.

Inclusivity is the capacity to welcome and facilitate the flow of people into and around the church, especially people who are disabled or have a disabling condition. Inclusivity means deliberately doing away with barriers that might impede entry or progress, whether those barriers are physical, emotional or spiritual. It means thinking about who might be inadvertently excluded by thoughtless or careless actions, words or attitudes.

Barrier bashing

I'm not talking here about steps, ramps or lifts. That's for Chapter 7: 'Inclusive buildings'. The barriers in this section may be less obvious to the untrained eye or ear. Let me run a few past you to get you thinking.

Academic barriers

A church in a university town or city may pride itself on the welcome it gives students, offering hospitality at church and at home with families, and the erudite, academic teaching that suits them so well. This church is indeed doing a marvellous job for students. However, if all the services and teaching or preaching are at the level of a university lecture, how will people cope who cannot follow such complex ideas or concentrate continually for 40 or 50 minutes? This is especially relevant if there are people with learning disabilities in the congregation, but you could argue that many others will also struggle with long or academic talks.

Invisible barriers

St Cuthbert's (a church somewhere in my imagination) has just had a makeover. A modern building, the inside is newly painted in tasteful magnolia, from floor to ceiling. What's more, the doors and frames are perfectly matched with satinwood magnolia: you can hardly tell they're there. Each door has a discreet notice revealing which room will be found inside.

You've probably guessed where this is leading. George, new to St Cuthbert's and partially sighted, walked round the church three times, looking for the door to the men's toilets. Eventually he had to ask.

Verbal barriers

The service has begun at St George's. 'Now we're going to worship in songs of praise. Everybody stand up!' cries the worship leader. One wheelchair user turns to her neighbour: 'I only wish I could!' I heard that exchange myself recently. This woman was lighthearted about it. Others might not be—especially if somebody then stands in front of them and blocks their view of the screen.

Social barriers

Many Christians are very friendly. Generally speaking, they feel good about their faith and about belonging to a church. Let's, for a moment, compare a church with a shop. (You'll see why shortly: hang in there!) In most shops you can go in, look around and select your shopping without having to talk to anybody. In some shops you can even avoid the checkout operator by using the self-scan option. Not so in church. The welcomer will want to shake your hand and enquire after your health. During the coffee time before or after the service, people will try to chat and get to know you. There may even be the 'sharing of the peace', when people shake hands or exchange a hug.

What's wrong with any of that? Nothing at all, if that suits your character and make-up, but, if you have autism, it could be a major barrier. If making eye contact, accepting physical touch, carrying on a casual conversation or having your personal space invaded is difficult for you, it's easy to see how threatening a place church could be.

No answers yet! How to deal with some of these issues is covered in Part 2—autism specifically in Chapter 9. The purpose of this section is to challenge thinking and help us to see with more alert eyes and minds.

Storytelling

Are you sitting comfortably? Then I'll begin. 'Once upon a time…'

Children love listening to stories, we know that—but so do most adults. The popularity of books, films and TV soaps is clear evidence. So why not include storytelling as a regular part of church? The Bible contains numerous stories of people and events, from creation and Adam and Eve to John's experience of heaven in the book of Revelation. They make fascinating reading and, if well told, can captivate listeners, drawing them into the situation, enabling them to identify with the characters, feel the emotions and understand the story more fully.

Some biblical accounts are a bit thin on detail, but the speaker can fill out the story by becoming familiar with the culture and habits of the time, reading other scriptures from the same period and using their imagination.

Not all Bible passages and subjects lend themselves to being expressed in story form, but it is a teaching method that can work well for any congregation. It can add variety and creativity to the church's teaching programme. Chapter 8, on learning disability, looks at storytelling in more detail, and some of the ideas there can be adapted for use with any congregation. You can use a first-person account, for example, in which the speaker takes the part of someone in the story, telling it from their perspective—such as Thomas reliving the moment when Jesus appeared to him and the other disciples in the upper room, dispelling his doubts; Peter recalling the astonishing events on the mount of transfiguration; or Simeon reflecting on his long wait for the Messiah and his eventual encounter with Mary, Joseph and the baby Jesus. An example of an accessible script is given in the Appendix (pp. 140–142).

Careful use of visual aids can be very helpful in getting a message across, and they don't have to be complicated or expensive. Jesus was a great one for visuals. In Matthew 6, during the Sermon on the Mount, he said, 'Look at the birds.' You can imagine him pointing up into the sky as he said it. He knew how to get people's attention and hold it. And do remember to describe anything that is purely visual for the benefit of those who cannot see.

One story Jesus told—the story of the prodigal son—would have shocked his audience in at least two places. When the younger son asks for his share of the estate, he is as good as saying to his father, 'I wish you were dead!' Then the son gets a job feeding pigs: for a Jewish boy that's horrifying. And when the son eventually arrives home, his father runs to meet him: it would be unheard-of for a family patriarch to do something so undignified. Oh, does that make three? Were you counting?

So what?

A good story, well told, can be educational, enjoyable and entertaining, but we need to do more than tell a story. In telling the story, we are creating a platform for teaching spiritual truth, so we need to find a way to apply the story appropriately and relevantly. The same story might be applied very differently to different congregations or groups of people. With a mixed group or congregation, two applications might be presented.

The application should be followed by an opportunity to respond. Some people need more time to think things through, so a period of quiet, a worship song or a sensitively led prayer may be helpful. Other possible responses might include taking a pebble and leaving it in a basket at the foot of the cross, writing or drawing a prayer on a card and attaching it to a prayer tree, or watching a series of images displayed on a screen.

Every-member ministry

Gone are the days when the minister did everything in a church. One vicar I spoke to said, 'I see my main job as encouraging, training and equipping other people to be effective so that more people can share the work and the church can grow.'

Chapter 1 introduced the idea that every Christian has a place in the body of Christ, and that each person has a valuable contribution to make to the life of their church or fellowship. While people with disabilities might need some help or support to attend or take part in services, we should also expect that their contribution to services and church life will be helpful and enriching. The person's gift may have nothing to do with their disability, yet they may need support to use the gift. The wheelchair user with a gift of leading in prayer may not be able to get to the lectern, but providing a radio microphone will set them free to use their gift.

Developing individual gifts and strengths

These days, there are courses for everything, run by churches, networks, denominations and organisations. If you want to be trained in an area of ministry, there will be a course not far away to attend. Quite often, people go on a course because it teaches something that they already do and want to do better, or it relates to a gift they recognise in themselves and want to develop. Some people, however, need help to discover what their gifts are. Sometimes other people can spot a gift before the person with the gift sees it. This is something we can do for our brothers and sisters with disabilities: look past the disability and seek to spot their gifts and potential for ministry. We can encourage people by commenting on what they do well and suggesting ways in which their gifts could be used.

Can-do people

There is a powerful principle at work here. If we take the trouble to get to know people, notice their gifts, encourage them and see their gifts develop and get used more widely in the church, do you know what happens? They become known for what they can do rather than what they can't do. The man whose legs don't work becomes Ron the cheerful welcomer; the woman with learning disabilities becomes a marvellous helper in children's church; the blind woman becomes Nessa the deacon. It's a universal principle: it works for us all. Don't you prefer to be known for what you can do rather than what you can't, or what you do well rather than the jobs you mess up?

Does God heal today?

'Jesus called his twelve disciples to him and gave them authority to drive out impure spirits and to heal every disease and illness' (Matthew 10:1).

Praying for healing has been a regular practice for Christians over the centuries. There have been numerous accounts of people being healed from major and minor illnesses, and of disabled people being healed from disabilities. Jennifer Rees-Larcombe was one, miraculously healed after eight years of pain and using a wheelchair.

Miracles do happen and God does heal, but evidently not always. The apostle Paul prayed over something that affected his body—perhaps a disability—but instead of healing him, God gave him these words: 'My grace is sufficient for you, for my power is made perfect in weakness' (2 Corinthians 12:9).

Jan Turner has been blind from birth and, for much of her adult life, lived with a back condition that required her to use a wheelchair. Then, after 23 years, God miraculously healed her back. Now she stands, walks and even jumps. Jan is still blind and regards that as an aspect of her identity. She is not expecting God to heal her sight. She is a wife, a mother, a church leader and much besides… and a blind person and, in Christ, a whole person.

Many disabled people have been upset by the well-meaning attempts of others to bring about their healing. A Bible promise is read or a prophetic word spoken, and healing is claimed in Jesus' name. Hopes are raised by the confidence of the prayer minister but then dashed if the person's condition remains unchanged. The hurt is compounded by the assumption, whether expressed or not, that they have not been healed because they do not have enough faith. A mature faith accepts that God has a good plan for each of us and knows best in all circumstances. As Daniel's three friends put it, 'If we are thrown into the blazing furnace, the God we serve is able to deliver us from it, and he will deliver us from Your Majesty's hand. But even if he does not, we want you to know, Your Majesty, that we will not serve your gods or worship the image of gold you have set up' (Daniel 3:17–18).

Jesus set the example in Matthew 20:32. Shouted at by two blind men whose persistent cries carried over the crowd's rebukes, Jesus asked them, 'What do you want me to do for you?' If a disabled person comes forward for prayer, it's easy to fall into the trap of assuming they want prayer for healing from their disability—but they are just as likely to be seeking prayer for the same sort of issues that affect any of us. The best advice is to follow Jesus' example and ask what they would like you to pray for. It is consistent with good practice and with the golden rule, 'Assume nothing; always ask.'

Real wholeness for anyone is found only through the salvation that comes through faith in Jesus Christ.

Celebrating difference

Every so often, the service leader at our church thanks the people who have been involved for their contribution, recognising speakers, readers and people who have led children's groups or worship, and giving thanks not only to them but to God who has given the gifts they've been using. It's good to acknowledge that we are all different, and in that difference lies our strength. So why not celebrate the difference more deliberately from time to time? Create an opportunity for people to interact with each other using words such as, 'I'm really glad that you are you!' or 'Did you know that you are fearfully and wonderfully made?'

There are great benefits to the church in this. If we create, by our attitudes, our openness and our love for each other, an atmosphere in which people can relax, they will be released into freedom to be themselves, and will be better able to develop into the people that God wants them to be. If people are given freedom to worship as God leads them, others may also be set free to worship in ways they may not have tried before. One person using a flag in worship can inspire a dozen others, creating something that is beautiful, worshipful and honouring to God.

The last word

We need to encourage people to come and worship the Lord and give him praises.

LESLEY BIFFEN

Chapter 5
Inclusive language

The Bible reading was Acts 2:42–47. The members of the congregation nodded approvingly as the pastor spoke of how the early church had everything in common, lent each other things, shared food and possessions and provided generously for people who were in need. That's what church should be like.

There was a new younger couple at church that day. Jean was blind but walked around the church confidently, holding on to Max's arm. During coffee after the service, Dorothy found out that they had not been married long and had just moved into a house round the corner from the senior elder. They had very little money, certainly not enough to afford a holiday this year. But they'd noticed the caravan on the senior elder's driveway. They'd been excited by the pastor's talk: did it mean they might be able to borrow the caravan so that they could have a holiday this year after all?

The senior elder has asked to meet with the pastor to seek advice.

For a while, I had a recurring nightmare. I was in a big church, about to preach, only to realise that I had done no preparation and had nothing to say. How embarrassing! Many people have a fear of embarrassing themselves by saying something that will offend or upset others. This can be a worry for a non-disabled person when speaking with or about people with disabilities.

Finding appropriate language to use may include using terms that are politically correct. However, our aim should be to select language that is positive and to avoid terminology that reinforces negative or incorrect assumptions and stereotypes. In the 1980s and earlier, it was common practice to refer to disabled people as having a physical or a mental handicap. Some say that the word 'handicap' has its origins in the phrase 'cap in hand' and carries implications of begging and reliance on charity. It is now universally rejected.

Most disabled people are used to seeing others struggle to find appropriate language to use, and are often less concerned about the words used than the attitude that lies behind them. They will forgive your ignorance, especially if you ask for their help to clarify what language and words are most appropriate and helpful and are part of their own vocabulary.

This vast resource—the wisdom and opinion of disabled people—is sadly underused. Disabled people are in a unique position to give advice and guidance. So, for example, if you're doing an access audit of your church or planning new buildings, be sure to include at least one disabled person on the team.

A key issue when thinking about disabled people is to remember that they are people first, people who happen to have a disability. Take care not to slip into a lazy way of talking by using expressions like 'the disabled', 'the blind' or 'the autistic'. Such expressions are impersonal, almost depersonalising the individual. Refer instead to the disabled person, the blind man, or the woman with autism.

The political correctness movement has served to make us think carefully about the language we use. It goes without saying that we do not wish to be offensive or appear careless in our spoken or written communication. However, political correctness can go too far by trying to avoid any negative words completely, replacing them with complicated or obscure ideas. 'Differently abled' and 'intellectually challenged' could, after all, refer to a jack-of-all-trades and a Mastermind contestant.

One useful guideline is to use words accurately and carefully. Quite often, on news bulletins, I have heard reports of 'a woman suffering from Down's Syndrome' or a man who was 'wheelchair-bound'. She wasn't suffering! She just had Down's Syndrome. Nor was the man tied in: he was a wheelchair user.

Through the Roof, a Christian charity working with disabled people, offers some good advice on language to avoid and what to say instead. This is contained in the table 'What do we say?' at the end of this chapter.

Jargon-free

'Jargon-free church? You might as well ask for a smoke-free bonfire or a wave-free ocean!' some people may say. 'It comes with the territory.'

Jargon is language that is understood by people who are 'in the know' but is meaningless or confusing to others. Nicodemus should have been in the know but was clearly thrown by Jesus' words about being 'born again' (John 3:3). In a conversation I had with a man with Down's Syndrome, who clearly had a real and profound faith in Christ, he mentioned more than once that he had been born again. I decided to ask him what being born again meant, and gave him time to think about the answer. He didn't know. He'd been told he'd been born again and he knew it was a good thing. That was enough for him.

One of the ways we can help people to feel relaxed and 'at home' is to use ordinary, everyday words as much as possible. Language that is 'churchy' and flowery can create a formality that inhibits participation. It may be worth thinking through the expressions that could be simplified or put into more down-to-earth words. It could be a benefit to everyone.

- What we say: We're going to move into a time of prayer.
- What we mean: Let's talk to God.

- What we say: Let's bring our petitions to the throne of grace.
- What we mean: Let's talk to God.

- What we say: There will be fellowship and refreshments after the service.
- What we mean: There will be tea and biscuits and time to chat after the service.

- What we say: Prayer ministry will be available during the next song.
- What we mean: If you'd like someone to pray with you, go to the back during this song.

- What we say: If you'd rather not receive the elements, come forward nonetheless for a blessing.
- What we mean: If you'd rather not take Communion today, please still come forward with everyone else. We'd like to pray that God will bless you.

Simple, not simplistic

The unfolding of your words gives light; it gives understanding to the simple. (PSALM 119:130)

I love the dynamic of this verse—the idea of prising open a scrunched-up ball of paper to reveal what's written there. As the eye focuses and dwells on what is written, the words begin to make sense. I do not understand the description of 'the simple' in the pejorative sense of 'uneducated' or 'foolish'. To me it means those who come with an open mind, prepared to accept God's word at face value, hungry for God to speak to them through it.

Many people in church congregations come from a cultural background in which English is a second or third language. Some may still be taking English lessons. Some people may have limited vocabulary and communication skills. These, as well as people with learning and other disabilities, will all benefit from clear and simple language in service leading, teaching, prayer and conversations.

The language issue is tackled more thoroughly in Chapter 8, on learning disability. For people with learning disabilities, the key access issue is access to truth. Many people with learning disabilities have limited vocabulary and comprehension, so the use of complex language makes teaching and worship much more difficult for them to follow. However, my experience is that the discipline of distilling scriptural truth and Christian teaching into straightforward, accessible language develops skills that will help all listeners to understand and engage more fully with the subject.

What do we say?

Through the Roof offers good advice on language to avoid and what to say instead:

Don't say cripple	Say disabled person
Don't say invalid	Say disabled person
Don't say handicapped	Say disabled person
Don't say mentally retarded	Say person with learning disabilities
Don't say mentally handicapped	Say person with learning disabilities
Don't say deaf aid	Say hearing aid
Don't say deaf loop	Say hearing loop
Don't say the disabled	Say disabled people
Don't say spastic	Say person with cerebral palsy
Don't say suffering from…	Say person with…
Don't say victim of…	Say person with…
Don't say afflicted by…	Say person with…
Don't say confined to a wheelchair	Say wheelchair user
Don't say wheelchair-bound	Say wheelchair user

FROM THROUGH THE ROOF'S 'BE A ROOFBREAKER', USED WITH PERMISSION

The last word

Jesus loves me for who I am, not what I am.
LESLEY BIFFEN

Chapter 6
Inclusive church life

'Item 4,' said the pastor, 'the nursery project. The architect's plans have been approved and the town council has agreed a grant towards start-up costs. The nursery will benefit many families on the estate, especially those that have children with special educational needs. For the project to go ahead, the church needs to agree the proposal to replace fixed pews with chairs to give space and flexibility. Are there any comments before we vote on it?'

Albert Jennings spoke first. 'I'm not sure we should get rid of those pews,' he said. 'They were donated in memory of our founding elder in 1887.'

The debate went on long into the night as opinions for and against were aired.

Chapter 4 dealt primarily with how to make church services more inclusive, considering how teaching and worship can be made more accessible and looking at how disabled people can be included—and, more than that, how they can use their God-given gifts to bless others and strengthen the church. This chapter takes a look at other aspects of church life and asks the question, 'How accessible are they?'

Small groups

The 'cell church' model revolves around small groups; they are the place where most learning happens and where people grow in their faith and understanding. Most churches see house groups or home groups as a vital part of church life where people develop strong and supportive relationships, praying and studying the Bible together among friends.

What would need to be done differently to make these group meetings inclusive for people with disabilities? Generalising for this kind of setting is not easy, as every disabled person is unique. Any changes or adaptations must be made to meet the individual's needs within the setting of the group, but some things are more obvious than others.

- A blind person may need a table on which to place a coffee mug or Bible. If she or he is a Braille reader, the Bible may be quite big. It's also a good idea to have everyone say their name at the start of the meeting so that a person with sight loss knows who is there and where they are sitting.
- Some people who are shy or have a mental illness may be quiet or passive in meetings. Leaders will need to be sensitive about drawing them into the conversation, ensuring that they feel valued, not threatened.
- A new group member in a wheelchair may need ramped or level access and an accessible toilet. Few homes have these facilities, so a change of venue could be considered.
- Someone with reduced hearing may cope well with Bible study if people speak one at a time and clearly. Prayers may be more difficult, though, as many people lower their voices and their heads when they pray.

People with learning disabilities have been happily included in home groups where a good balance has been found between simplifying content to include the individual and retaining sufficient challenge for other group members. Some churches run special groups for adults with learning disabilities, to address the issues of language and concentration span.

There is one generalisation that can be applied, and that's to do with attitudes. If the group has an attitude that says, 'Everybody's welcome. We'll do what it takes to make sure you fit in and enjoy being here!' then it's very likely that it will work. The newcomer will sense the warmth of a supportive and welcoming group.

That same generalisation applies right across the church's activities, whatever they may be. A church with the attitude 'We want to be accessible and to make people feel included' will be creative in finding ways for that to happen, providing successful solutions to tricky dilemmas.

The Alpha course

Alpha and other introductions to Christianity have proved effective for many people with disabilities. The usual practical issues need to be thought through, and care taken over choice of food if guests have limited arm movement or special dietary requirements. However, the Alpha talks are long if the DVDs are used, and are not at all suitable for people with learning disabilities. To address this issue, an accessible version of the course has been developed and is available from Prospects. Torch Trust offers Braille editions of the Alpha resources, including the leaders' book.

Bible conferences

Whether it's Spring Harvest, the Keswick Convention, New Wine or Soul Survivor, many people enjoy an occasional or even annual excursion to the Bible Week of their choice. It's a chance to be spiritually challenged and refreshed and to spend time relaxing with family or friends, enjoying teaching and worship that are a bit different from those encountered in the home church.

For several years, I worked with Spring Harvest as disability consultant for one of their site weeks at Minehead or Skegness. That showed me two things. First, I saw how hard the event leaders work to make Spring Harvest accessible to all (and I know other events do, too). They provide signers, ramped access to marquees, speech to text, trained team members for children with additional needs, celebrations for adults with learning disabilities and much more. Second, it showed me how difficult it can be to meet every individual's needs. Problems arise sometimes because of mistakes, and other times because there are multiple needs within one family.

One man in a wheelchair was upset because fixed seating arrangements meant that he was initially not able to sit with his wife. She was deaf so she needed to sit in the area close to the BSL signers, but this area was not accessible for wheelchairs. We solved the problem by putting a camera on the signer and installing an extra screen in an area where they could sit together.

A young autistic man found the youth venue difficult to cope with: there were loud noises, many people and sudden changes in the pace of the meetings. Supported by one of the 'special needs' team, he eventually settled at the back of the venue where it was less busy and quieter, joining in when it suited him. In this way he benefited from both teaching and worship.

One family arrived to find that their accommodation was on the first floor, completely inaccessible to their disabled relative. We negotiated with Butlins for them to have a ground floor unit instead. No accommodation of the same standard was available, so they were upgraded to a Gold Standard chalet at no extra cost, which more than compensated for the inconvenience and initial upset.

If your church is encouraging people to go to a particular Bible Week, you can check in advance how accessible the event is:

- Ring or email the event office, being specific about the needs of any disabled people. The organisers may need time to make suitable arrangements.
- A disabled person may need someone else (another guest) to act as an 'enabler', committed to giving them help with daily routines and getting round the event.
- Disabled children usually need to be registered in advance so that they can be properly supported in their age group.
- If you are taking people with learning disabilities, check that the event has meetings arranged for them so that they can benefit fully from the week.
- If adapted or accessible accommodation is needed, ask for a full description of the facilities.
- Event programmes will often have a note of how accessible each venue is.
- Some events offer discounts to people who are in receipt of certain benefits.

I have spoken to countless people with disabilities who have had a great time at major events. With your encouragement and support, many more will do so too.

Social events

The harvest supper, beach party, picnic and games in the park, or barn dance—they can all be made inclusive. One obvious issue is to make sure people get invited. It's not enough for the notice to appear in the church news sheet. If people don't read, they may never get to know about the event at all. Some people will need to be invited personally to give them the confidence to come. They may also need a lift to get there.

Some people might say that a barn dance and people with disabilities just don't go together. I can assure you from experience that they do! Wheelchair users may dance in their chair or may be looking for an energetic pusher to keep them moving (that's where I can usually be found at a barn dance), and, where the dancers include people with learning disabilities, choosing easier dances will help the evening go with a swing.

Service with a smile

I often hear the welcome words, 'Anything you want me to do?' Chris has a learning disability and a desire to help. When I'm setting up for a meeting or have things to carry in from the car, Chris is always the first to offer and sticks with the job until it's finished.

Around a church, there are always jobs to be done—cleaning, gardening, painting, maintenance, typing, administration, serving in the church café or shop—a hundred practical tasks. There may well be some jobs that a disabled person can't do, but almost certainly there will be things they can achieve and would love to help with. For those who have time and who want to help, finding ways for them to serve will bring wide-ranging benefits.

Evangelists

Many people with disabilities have wonderful creative gifts and are skilled in music, craft or speaking. Many are able to share the gospel message powerfully and can be very effective in outreach and evangelism.

Singer-songwriter Marilyn Baker, who is blind, has inspired

countless people through her songs, which are full of scriptural truth and Spirit-filled wisdom. She continues to encourage thousands of people every week through the *Reflections* programme on Premier Radio and the RNIB's 'Insight' broadcasting channel.

A group of people with learning disabilities from St Peter's Church in Hampshire regularly lead church services across the county, using drama, testimony, signing, worship and prayer to share the gospel message. One song in their repertoire is popular wherever they go. It contains only five words, repeated again and again, rather like a Taizé chant: 'The Father himself loves you'. As members of the group move around the church, shaking people's hands and singing to them 'The Father himself loves you', it has a profound effect. The simplicity of the message and the direct and uninhibited way in which it is shared often touch people at an emotional level.

A mountainous dilemma

You may like to know that writing this chapter has presented me with a real challenge. Let me explain. For 20 years I have been taking groups of up to 35 men from my church for a walking weekend in the Brecon Beacons, South Wales, each September. Quite early on, we began allowing for differences in fitness and enthusiasm for scaling the peaks: we always have a choice of walks on offer. There's the opportunity of twelve miles over the tops for the 'yompers', four miles along the canal with refreshment stops for our 'gentlemen walkers', and usually something in between as a modest challenge. The weekends are popular and enjoyable—but I've never had a wheelchair user ask to come.

Here's the challenge for me: could we make it possible? Why shouldn't a wheelchair user enjoy a weekend in the Brecons with other men, experiencing the fresh air, beautiful scenery, camaraderie and fun, not to mention the good food? We'd need to find some fully accessible routes and a few people willing to take a turn at pushing, but why not? It's a challenge I'm ready to embrace.

The last word

What I love about the Prospects Group is that they always have fun. I love singing his praises.

LESLEY BIFFEN

Chapter 7
Inclusive buildings

'So that's agreed,' announced the church secretary. 'We put an accessible loo in the deacons' room and they get a cupboard in the store room instead.' 'But, but...' stammered deacon Bill Rawlins. 'No buts!' the pastor interrupted. 'You should have been at the church meeting last week. The vote was unanimous. Anyway, it's a better use of what little space we've got.'

'And the wheelchair access question,' continued the church secretary, 'was solved by agreeing to a ramp at the kitchen door with access via the path along the side and back of the church. That gives level access to every part of the church, and at half the price of a ramp at the front entrance. Great result!'

'Hang on a minute,' said Hannah Rawlins. 'Don't you think that might make Michael feel a bit like a second-class citizen, having to use the back door?'

'Ah,' said the pastor. 'I do wish you'd been here to mention that last week.'

Buildings—here we are at last! But why, you may ask, have we had to wait until Chapter 7 to think about inclusive buildings? Is building accessibility not important?

On the contrary, making our church buildings accessible is very important. It is vital that our premises and facilities work really well for everyone who uses them now and will do so in the future. The reason this chapter comes last in Part 1 is that, however important buildings are, people matter more. We can have the most accessible building with every state-of-the-art facility but, if the people of the church have attitudes and an approach that make disabled people feel uncomfortable or second-class, the excellence of the building will not compensate. Negative attitudes will undermine the message of accessibility that the building appears to give.

Good buildings are a tool, a facility that will help the church achieve its mission—making it a great place in which to welcome newcomers and worship together, and from which to send people out to fulfil the great commission to make disciples.

There are two significant pieces of legislation that have come into force in recent years: the Disability Discrimination Act of 1995 and the Equality Act of 2010. A summary of these, with links, is given later in this chapter. The Acts deal with both practical and attitudinal issues and will affect churches in different ways according to local conditions, the size of the church, the restrictions of the building and site, listed buildings issues, and so on. Many of their requirements are moderated by what is reasonable in a particular case. Often the requirements of the law constitute a minimum standard, while many churches will have already gone way beyond what is specified in the Acts.

As we look at current legislation, we should be conscious of a 'kingdom law' that predates our laws by 2000 years. The scriptures mentioned in earlier chapters make clear God's intention that no one should be excluded from the opportunity to worship. As churches work towards compliance with that command, they will almost certainly find that they meet or even exceed the requirements of current legislation.

Before going into detail, some levels of accessibility are sensible for any church to try and achieve, regardless of whether there are disabled people who need them this very weekend. With an ageing population, the number of people with impaired mobility, hearing and sight is on the increase. We will do well to be prepared. Perhaps you have no wheelchair users at present? One of the church pensioners (or children) may take a tumble, break a leg and turn up in a borrowed chair, expecting to get in. A ramped or level entrance, with handrails beside any steps or ramps, will make access easier for families with pushchairs, musicians with arms full of gear, people with sticks or walking frames—oh, and wheelchair users, of course.

An induction or hearing loop will help people whose hearing is augmented by hearing aids. It's just a cable round the room connected via a small unit to the amplification system, and is not very expensive to buy and fit. You may not know whether there are 'customers' for the loop, as hearing aids may be hidden in the ear or under hair, but I can tell from my own experience that a working loop can make the difference between full involvement and understanding, and a feeling of frustration and isolation.

Blindness and visual impairment are covered in detail in Chapter 10. However, it is reasonable to expect a church to have one or two copies of a large-print Bible and songbooks. The guidance from Torch Trust is that, if song words are projected but not provided in a book, they should be made available in large print. There will almost always be somebody who chooses to use it.

This chapter would be incomplete without mention of the accessible toilet. It needs to be, at the minimum, big enough for someone to transfer comfortably from a wheelchair on to the toilet, and ideally big enough for a second person to give help or support. Comprehensive diagrams, design specifications and guidelines for creating an accessible toilet can be found at www.accesscode.info/buildings.

Legislation

Disability Discrimination Act 1995

The essential elements of the Act are as follows.

- It is unlawful to treat a disabled person 'less favourably' for a reason related to their disability:
  - By refusal or non-provision of service
  - In the standard or manner of service
  - In the terms of service
- Service providers are required to make 'reasonable adjustments' for disabled people. For example:
  - Change practices, policies or procedures
  - Provide auxiliary aids or services
  - Find a way of avoiding a physical barrier to providing services
- There is an obligation to remove, alter or avoid a physical feature that acts as a barrier to providing a service to disabled people. What is reasonable depends on the cost of the alteration proposed, in relation to:
  - The resources the church has
  - The amount the church has already spent on alterations
  - The availability of financial assistance

Equality Act 2010

The introduction of the Equality Act removed none of the requirements of the Disability Discrimination Act, but added a number of additional categories of discrimination, such as associative discrimination, discrimination by perception and indirect discrimination. These apply primarily to employment situations rather than access issues, but they do tend to increase the expectation that reasonable steps will be taken to avoid putting a disabled person at a substantial disadvantage. You can find the legislation at these links:

- Equality Act: http://homeoffice.gov.uk/equalities
- Disability Discrimination Act: www.legislation.gov.uk/ukpga/2005/13/contents

Through the Roof has a comprehensive list of helpful links that cover buildings and access, together with links to organisations involved in all aspects of disability ministry: see www.throughtheroof.org/info-and-resources/links

The last word

I know for myself that the house of God is a friendly place.
LESLEY BIFFEN

Part 2

WELCOME!

Chapter 8
Including people with learning disabilities

'Learning disability' is a broad description covering dozens of specific conditions that may affect a person's ability to study and learn, to communicate, to gain life skills, to reason and to speak. Any or all of these abilities may be affected and a person may be categorised as having a mild, moderate or severe learning disability.

Known learning disabilities include Down's Syndrome, Fragile-X Syndrome, Rett Syndrome, Tourette's Syndrome, Angelman Syndrome, Prader-Willi Syndrome and dyspraxia. Cerebral palsy is not a learning disability, but some people with it also have a learning disability. Autism and other conditions on the autistic spectrum, such as Asperger Syndrome, are covered in Chapter 9. Some autistic people have learning disabilities; others are highly intelligent, independent people.

For more information about learning disabilities, see the links at the end of this chapter. A helpful factsheet is available from the British Institute of Learning Disabilities, and a description of many learning disability syndromes can be found on the About Learning Disabilities website.

The key issue: access to truth

Many people with learning disabilities also have another disability. Of the 20 members of the inclusive Bible study group

I'm part of, four are wheelchair users, two are blind, one has no speech and only five can get to the meetings without help from a friend. There is a wide range of ability within the group, but the common factor is a difficulty in understanding the language that is commonly used to talk about and explain Christianity.

The way we express Christian truth in teaching, preaching and worship is complex and often wordy, making it difficult for people with learning disabilities to follow. So the key access issue for people with learning disabilities is access to truth. Most other people with disabilities, once seated in church and able to see and/or hear, can get the message. For the majority of people with learning disabilities, that same message will pass them by; they may simply not understand it at all, or perhaps not enough for it to make sense.

This chapter looks at why that is the case and what can be done about it.

All at sea

A friend of mine was fond of telling a story about how she, herself the parent of a daughter with Down's Syndrome, fell into a language trap. She was having a bad morning, rushing to get ready to go out, and said to her daughter, 'Oh Christine, I'm all at sea today!' Christine replied, 'Oh no you're not, Mummy. You're right here in the kitchen with me!'

Metaphor and simile are very common in everyday speech and are widely used in Christian teaching, preaching and song writing. The difficulty is that many people with learning disabilities understand words at face value; they will take a metaphor literally. If a word has several meanings (or sound-alikes), they may settle for the one they're most familiar with.

Consider these words from a worship song by Dave Bilbrough:

All hail the Lamb,
enthroned on high,
his praise shall be
our battle cry.

DAVE BILBROUGH, COPYRIGHT © 1987 THANKYOU MUSIC*

People will be familiar with rain and hail (especially if they live in the UK), so this song may appear to be like a weather forecast. There is also a magnificent metaphor in 'His praise shall be our battle cry', but imagine reading it and not understanding the connection between praise and battles. Finally, however are people with learning disabilities going to understand the word 'lamb' in this context?

Words like 'salvation', 'repentance', 'ascension', 'anointing' and 'consecration' will all present a challenge to anyone new to church, and especially so for anyone with limited vocabulary and comprehension. Abstract ideas and concepts are also difficult for people with learning disabilities to grasp. Anything that requires them to imagine something they can't see, hear or touch is likely to be difficult. Forgiveness, the Trinity and being part of the body of Christ are abstract concepts. You could say that God himself is abstract; we know he's real, but most people never experience his impact on their lives in a physical sense.

Then there is the matter of concentration span. Some elements of church last for a relatively short time or don't require a high level of concentration. To get the most out of the sermon, however, you need to concentrate continuously for, well... how long is the sermon in your church?

One other issue that can put people at a disadvantage is that only about one-third of those with learning disabilities read well enough to follow a reading from the Bible or the song words projected on to a screen. Try putting yourself in the position of being unable to read. How well would you cope in church?

Thinking these things through and taking a few simple steps can prevent people with learning disabilities from being 'all at sea' in your church.

The Sunday service

You can help people with learning disabilities to relax and feel at home with everyone else on Sunday mornings (or whenever the church meets) by doing things like these:

- Create a relaxed and informal atmosphere in which it's OK for children and others to move around during the service if they need to, and where a little noise is not only tolerated but treated as normal.
- Bearing in mind that many people with learning disabilities do not read, make sure that you give any notices and directions during the service verbally and clearly. Don't rely on the newsletter or order of service to do your communicating.
- Include one or two songs with accessible words and tunes. It could be a song with an easy chorus, even if the verses are more difficult. Examples are 'Light of the world', with the chorus 'Here I am to worship', and 'The splendour of the king', with the chorus 'How great is our God'. In addition, Prospects offers a range of fully accessible song resources.
- Careful use of visual aids can help. Introducing a relevant object, picture or video clip could add meaning and renew attention span.
- If the sermon is more than 20 minutes, consider dividing it into two sections with a song in between.

- After the sermon, invite the preacher to conclude with a two-sentence summary. That way, people who may not have taken in the whole message will at least hear the key point that the speaker wants to make.
- If, in conversation after the service, you find that someone has not understood the sermon and wants to do so, offer to talk through it with them, or find someone else to do it.
- Make sure that preachers and other participants are prepared for members of the congregation to make impromptu comments and give audible answers to rhetorical questions.

Sarah's story

Sarah Redgrove has quite a story to tell. 'I don't mind people knowing that I struggled with church because of my learning disability. I just couldn't understand what people were talking about in church.'

Then she started going to a specially organised group at a church in partnership with Prospects. 'They helped me to learn about Jesus, how he died for us, and about forgiving everybody.'

As a result, Sarah became a Christian, but there was no similar group where she lived, so she began praying for one to start. In due course her prayers were answered and she became the founding member of the Prospects group in Lincoln.

Sarah was an extremely shy person, but being part of the group gradually built her confidence. Having attended the Grapevine event several times as a guest at the Prospects meetings there, she was invited to join the ministry team and has been involved in helping to lead the event several times.

She and her family are thrilled with the way she has grown in confidence over the years. On several occasions Sarah has undertaken public speaking engagements for Prospects, addressing up to 100 people in meetings at the Palace of Westminster.

Sarah's story illustrates the value of having a small group that specialises in working with people who have learning disabilities. Not only will this provide a setting where people can get to know Jesus for themselves and be discipled in their faith, but it will also enable them to develop skills, confidence and friendships that will open up a fuller participation in church and community life.

Asked how she would describe her relationship with Jesus, Sarah replied, 'I love him to bits!'

Preparing to welcome people

People with learning disabilities live in almost every community now. The days when they were concentrated in institutions that became the long-stay hospitals of the 20th century are, thankfully, over. Resettlement programmes have meant that most people with learning disabilities now live with parents or family members or in family-sized units supported by statutory, private or voluntary-sector providers. That makes it highly likely that they live near you or your church, shop at the same stores as you and frequent the same cinemas, swimming pools or cafés.

There are over 1.5 million people with learning disabilities in the UK, and they need to know that God loves them. Unless they come from a Christian family, they will probably never have heard about Jesus. There's a hidden mission field on the doorstep of every church, just waiting for you to do something about it.

What could you do? Put on a special event and invite people in, perhaps. You could approach the homes where people live and talk to the manager. Any events with food and an element of fun should be popular.

If that sounds scary, Prospects (www.prospects.org.uk)

can help you plan and prepare. It's not as difficult as you might imagine—but be careful. If people come and enjoy the experience, they might want to come back regularly! You may be wise to think ahead and plan to start running a regular Bible study/discipleship group. Again, Prospects can help. They have lots of resource materials for Bible study and worship, including the Easy-to-Read Bible and several collections of specially written worship songs. They can also advise you and run a training day to get you started.

Accessible drama and teaching

Drama is a powerful visual means of communication. One style of drama that can be very helpful and easy to create is spontaneous drama. Unrehearsed, people are invited to take part in walking through an incident recorded in scripture. As they act out the parts, people take in and understand the events better, remembering the story and its lessons too. It might sound to you like a recipe for disaster, but our experience in Prospects meetings is that it works extremely well and is thoroughly enjoyable.

A key factor is having a drama leader or narrator who is fully familiar with the Bible story and has a confident and relaxed manner.

The relevant section of the Bible is read first, then the leader introduces the drama and invites participation. Actors may have props or costumes to add atmosphere and colour. The narrator gives explanations and emphasises the key teaching points in the drama. Some dramas can include everyone in the meeting or congregation—for example, playing the opposing armies when David takes on Goliath, or the crowd listening to Jesus as he speaks from Peter's boat.

At the end of the drama, the actors are thanked and

applauded. The key points of the drama and Bible reading are drawn together afterwards with relevant application to people's lives.

'I was there'

A different kind of dramatic presentation is when the speaker plays the part of a character who was present at a biblical event, presenting an imaginary first-person account of the story. Such storytelling can be very powerful; an example is included in the Appendix at the back of this book.

For any piece of teaching, target ten minutes as your maximum duration; most people can cope with between five and ten minutes. If an application is to follow a piece of narrative teaching, put a song between the two parts, to help with concentration.

Churches that have done it

Does all this sound like a good thing to do? Be encouraged by some stories from churches that have given it a go and opened their doors and hearts to people with learning disabilities.

St Peter's Church, Yateley, in Hampshire, has had a Prospects Group for 20 years. The vicar, Revd Andy Edmunds, says:

The group is always well attended and all its members really look forward to meeting together. They share their faith and love for God with simplicity and enthusiasm, without inhibition. When one suffers, their support for each other is sincere and sensitive, but, for most of the time, it is just great fun and a joy to be a part of. Most of the group members also have active roles within the church, welcoming, serving refreshments, leading in prayer and in other ways. Together they bring variety and spontaneity to services and make a valuable contribution to church community life.

Norman Green leads the Prospects Group at Rugby Evangelical Free Church.

Nine years ago, our church, a very conservative evangelical church in the Reformed tradition, began a Prospects ministry group. Up to that time, we had had no contact with people with learning disabilities and none attended our services. The monthly meeting of our group, which has about 15 members, is also attended regularly by several people who are not members of the leadership team. They appreciate not only the simple style of the meeting but also the warmth of the fellowship. We all find that we receive far more from our group members than we ever give. Today, two women with learning disabilities regularly attend our church services. Many of the group also come to church social activities and clearly feel quite at home. We believe we have a long way to go in making our church more inclusive, but a start has been made.

Good conversations: a few tips

Bearing in mind some of the comments made earlier about language, here are a few guidelines and tips about conversations with people who have learning disabilities.

- Allow time for the conversation. Avoid giving the impression that you need to get on to do something else.
- Give the person your full attention, and listen. Give yourself time to get used to the person's voice.
- Use the same kind of words that they use. Limit your vocabulary if you need to, but don't speak down to people or use patronising or childish language.
- If you can't understand what's being said, don't be afraid or embarrassed to ask the person to repeat it.

- If the person has come with a carer, helper or family member, try to have as much of the conversation as possible with the person, involving the supporter when necessary or as appropriate.
- Don't be afraid of silences; you may need to wait for an answer. Don't be tempted to finish people's sentences for them.

Useful links

- Mencap: www.mencap.org.uk
- About Learning Disabilities: www.aboutlearningdisabilities. co.uk
- The Foundation for People with Learning Disabilities: www. learningdisabilities.org.uk
- Prospects: www.prospects.org.uk
- BILD, the British Institute of Learning Disabilities: www. bild.org.uk
- Down's Syndrome Association: www.downs-syndrome.org. uk
- Baptist Union Initiative with People with Learning Disabilities: www.baptist.org.uk/prayer

The last word

I love Prospects because they help people to learn about Jesus.
LESLEY BIFFEN

Chapter 9
Including people with autism

This chapter was written by Ann Memmott, an adult on the autism spectrum who advises churches on autism inclusion. As you read, imagine it is Ann speaking to you. When she says 'we' or 'us', she is referring to people with autism (more than half a million in the UK), a group of which she is part.

Autism is one of the most common disabilities. One in 100 people is on the autism spectrum, which includes Asperger Syndrome. 'Classic autism' is a combination of autism and a learning disability, whereas Asperger Syndrome is now believed to be autism but without a learning disability. Everything in this chapter is a generalisation, as everyone will be somewhat different.

Autism is a brain design difference. As far as we know, it happens before birth, and no one knows why. Our brains are wired to be excellent at specialised tasks but are fairly hopeless at understanding social relationships. It's often a very mixed blessing. We're on average ten times more accurate than other people, but the bits of the brain that 'decode' people's behaviour, gestures, facial expressions, eye contact and tone of voice aren't wired up very well.

We can struggle to understand non-verbal meanings, so we often need really clear explanations to tell us how someone is feeling. We can also struggle to use body language and tone of voice to tell others how we're feeling. We cannot always understand complicated language or long sentences or metaphors. We are, however, hugely loyal, honest people who make splendid friends once you win our trust. We're often great seekers of social justice, able to work painstakingly towards a better future for everyone. Some of us are church leaders and church advisers. Many of us have a huge range of good speech, but no clue how to use it to persuade others to like us and support our work. That lack of social understanding and our social 'clumsiness' is the problem. Being able to speak is one thing. Knowing what to say and what not to say—that's the important bit. We improve with time and practice and good friends guiding us on the rules. We can be very direct in what we say, but it's not meant to be rude or sound aggressive.

We may also stand too close to people because we can't see them properly and can't work out how far away we are. It's not meant in a threatening way. Some on the autism spectrum may seek a reassuring hug or hand-holding. This should not be seen as either intimacy or threat. It is often because our brains don't produce a chemical called oxytocin, which helps people to use social skills and stay calm. The comfortable pressure of, say, a blanket wrapped around us, or safe and agreed touch, can boost the chemical. But if people touch us unexpectedly, it can really hurt, because of our heightened skin sensitivity. Always ensure that you ask permission and are sensible, open and safe with the use of touch.

People on the autism spectrum have a huge need to know what's going to happen that day and in what order. Eight out of ten of us also have sensory processing difficulties. If someone is blind, it means they cannot see enough. If they are deaf, it means they cannot hear enough. With autism, we may see, hear, feel, smell and taste too much, all the time. It's an avalanche of information from our senses, and our brains aren't good at working out what's important information and what's not.

Eight out of ten of us think visually rather than in words, which means that we try to visualise what a word looks like or what someone would be doing. This is why metaphors and expressions can be such a struggle for us.

We may use repetitive body movements or sounds ('stimming'), such as rocking back and forth or hand-flapping or repeating a particular sound. It may seem odd, but it helps us to know where our bodies are, and helps us to cope. If it's not disruptive, it's not a problem.

We often prefer to make friends with just one or two people, because big groups are such hard work for our brains. If those friends aren't there, we can find being in a bigger group quite stressful and may need extra reassurance.

We autistic people are all individuals, having our own interests, loves and dislikes, as do other people—but we also have those few differences. In summary, we're not good at automatically coping with social situations, coping with random events or coping in busy, bright, noisy places for long. Sooner or later our brain wiring overheats, which means we need time out to let it cool down again. If that happens, we need a quiet space away from other people, no fuss or social conversation, and the chance to just 'be' for a while. The offer of a blanket or coat to wrap round us helps us if we're in a panic.

Here are some myths debunked:

- Autistic people are not all like Rain Man from that film. In fact, very of us few are. Most will seem to be completely 'ordinary'. Everyone is an individual, with their own personality, level of intelligence, likes, dislikes and abilities. Very few of us have amazing recall.

- It's not all about boys and men. Many of us are girls or women.
- Only one in ten has a learning disability as well.
- It's the same prevalence rate of autism for adults as it is for children. We don't grow out of it, although we can learn how to cope better as an adult.
- Autism is not caused by parenting problems.
- It's not about 'disruptive behaviour': most of us are kind, gentle and very rule-abiding. But because we're the quiet ones, people don't realise we're autistic too. Disruptive behaviour happens rarely, and is almost always caused by sensory pain or fear of the unknown. Finding the cause can solve the problem.
- We don't often lack empathy. If people tell us that they are sad, we can then know that they are sad and do something about it. The problem is that we can't see it from their faces or hear it from their tone of voice. We learn empathy through careful years of practice and because we really do care about the people in our lives.

Are there autistic people in the Bible? I think there are. For example, Nicodemus is one of my favourite characters, and I think he may well have been autistic. We meet him in the Gospel of John, chapter 3. He was a Jewish leader, and a brain that could understand every detail of the law would have been highly prized for that role. He approached Jesus in the quiet of the evening, away from the crowds. He didn't understand the metaphor about being 'born again'. He reached for a rule-book to try to stop Jesus being crucified, rather than using social reasoning. At the tomb, he turned up with a simply huge amount of herbs—a bit of a social faux pas, I reckon. Yet clearly he was a friend of Jesus and was there for him even at the tomb. Jesus didn't try to cure him, either.

What do we mean by an 'inclusive church' for people with autism? What are the benefits of it?

My team looked at the churches who had declared that they would welcome people on the autism spectrum. The overall numbers in their congregations kept rising year after year. Why? Well, we can't be sure, but a church that is welcoming for autistic people is also welcoming for everyone else. What helps us also helps just about everyone, we've found. So it's a win–win situation for churches to include us wherever they can.

Here are some comments from participants in a regular Bible study group set up by a member of the clergy team who is on the autism spectrum:

We wouldn't know what we'd do without the group that you run… It gives everyone a chance to have a say, with no censorship or controlling issues, so that people feel able to voice their opinion without fear of ridicule… You're a breath of fresh air.

A church leader who had welcomed and included an autistic woman, despite initial concerns about whether it would work, said this:

You have added so much to this church over the last two years—it is an absolute blessing to have you among us.

And this is a comment from a parishioner, on hearing a sermon by a church leader on the autism spectrum:

This is a wonderful sermon, and—if I may say so—just what I need to hear afresh myself at a time when I'm finding it very hard to forgive various people.

So often, 'inclusive' stops at, 'We will let you sit in our church during worship, but we won't treat you as a friend or let you help.' Sometimes fear, based on lack of knowledge of autism, is behind this attitude. We all have gifts to bring to God and to our church communities. Some have leadership skills, pastoral gifts or prayer ministry to offer. Some will have talents for singing, music, doing the church accounts or running the website. Some will be excellent at policies and committee work. Some will enjoy taking part in the services in some role, or making new disciples. Some contribute a lot in charities and community work. Every person with autism has much to offer as a friend and fellow companion in this journey of faith. Some will manage church life without assistance; others would welcome a little support. Do ask what might help.

Inclusive language and materials

- Think about the words used in worship—for example, 'Thou art in heaven'. For the eight out of ten of us on the autism spectrum who think visually, our brains might see an image of someone doing some artwork in heaven. 'Take a seat' might well result in us picking one up, since that's exactly what you'd do if you were taking a seat somewhere! The use of language needs to be careful. Keep sentences short. Think about whether you can explain metaphors and expressions. Jesus did.
- Think about your website. It will be really helpful to have a map on there to show where you are, as well as pictures of who's who. Photos of the car parking area, entrance, outside and inside of the church building will help, and how to find a loo. That sort of detail encourages us autistic people to visit and find out about you. Keep wording simple and clear.

- Think about your newsletters. Use pictures and diagrams rather than just lots of words.
- Think about materials you use in the service or in home group sessions. Is there a way to make it really clear and easier to read? Is there someone who can help explain things, if someone asks for help?
- Some people on the autism spectrum are not able to speak and will use pictures or sign language methods to communicate, or iPads or similar electronic devices. It can be great fun to join in with this and find ways to include autistic people in conversations and events using those things.

Inclusive church life

Being part of a Christian community is not just about going to church once a week. It's about how you also encourage people with autism to join Bible study groups or home groups, help run junior church or services, do pastoral work or join the choir or music group. Autistic people may be able to help with fêtes and fundraising, sit on or run committees, or have the skills to lead a church or train for ministry. Certainly there are ministers, priests, vicars and even bishops in the country who are on the autism spectrum.

Social events and occasions—how to involve people

People on the autism spectrum find social occasions very exhausting and bewildering. We're not antisocial. We just find it so hard to know what to say and do that we end up afraid to join in. Our brains also cannot pick out just one voice in a background of lots of other voices; we don't have that bit of the brain wired in properly. It will be really helpful to let us know lots and lots of detail about the event. Let us bring a good friend or relative, or ask if we would like someone in the congregation to be our friend during that event. Give us the chance to do a task rather than just stand and chat. Don't hold events in echoing noisy spaces: an outside or heavily carpeted space can be better, where possible.

Buildings and spaces

Because of our different sensory systems, it's hugely important to get buildings and spaces right. Faulty or flickering overhead lighting is often like being under a strobe light for many of us, and might be as much of a hazard as it would be for someone with epilepsy. We can hear such detail in background noise that electronic equipment humming, or background traffic and aircraft noise, may mean that we don't hear people properly. Perfumes and scents from flowers can be overwhelming, and we may try to sit away from them. It really helps to have a non-echoing space that has lots of natural daylight without strong shadows. A north-facing room with big windows can be ideal— or the chance to retreat to a quieter room from time to time.

Children on the autism spectrum

Everything mentioned above also applies to children on the autism spectrum. There will be a huge need for routine and predictability, for the support of a safe person whom they can really trust, for understandable and very clear materials, and for a space that is free from flickering lights and lots of echoing, confusing noise.

Don't expect eye contact. It really hurts and frightens children on the autism spectrum to make eye contact with others, because it's wired into the wrong bit of the brain.

Do use really clear instructions. 'I'm wondering what Jesus was thinking' isn't an instruction, so most children on the autism spectrum won't realise that you are asking them to contribute. 'Stand and sing with me' will result in the child joining you on the stage, not just standing up and singing. After all, you said to go and sing 'with you'. The world becomes a very confusing place when you speak in expressions and use body language to convey meaning, and the children have no idea what you mean.

If you are planning away days and weekends with youth groups, take good advice from parents and carers as well as talking with the child. The change of routine and unpredictability of a new venue can be overwhelming for some children on the autism spectrum, but good planning, and maybe an advance visit to the site, can help a great deal. A caring known supporter, helper or friend can be a blessing, too. Children on the autism spectrum can bring so much to these events in friendship and thoughtful contribution. It's worth the effort.

Resources and links

- www.oxford.anglican.org/social-justice/disability/ welcoming-those-with-autism-and-asperger-syndrome-in-our-churches-and-communities.html
- www.churchofengland.org/media/39672/gs1725.pdf is the Opening the Doors report to Synod on learning disability and autism
- www.autism.org.uk/living-with-autism/out-and-about/ religion-going-to-place-of-worship.aspx contains information from the National Autistic Society

Chapter 10
Including people with sight loss

This chapter was written by Dr Mike Townsend. Mike, who is blind, is chair of Through the Roof and a trustee of Torch Trust, Royal National Institute of Blind People and Guide Dogs. Throughout his adult life Mike has striven for the spiritual, emotional and physical well-being of people with sight loss and for their full inclusion in the life of the church.

Surveys show that the most feared of disabilities is sight loss.

Vic ran a thriving engineering business in Leicester. He loved driving out to customers and enjoyed seeing their satisfaction with his work. One morning he woke up and could see nothing. The room span. Vic got out of bed and fell on the floor.

'I was terrified. Even my bed didn't feel safe.'

Sudden and complete sight loss is unusual. I lost my sight when I was eight. There were slight problems with my sight, which an experimental operation failed to correct. For a while I was surrounded by tall white looming figures—the medical and school staff—and I was removed from my family and sent away for special education. Through partially sighted eyes, the world was a frightening place. Then all my sight went. They said it was a 'sympathetic reaction' within my eyes. It didn't seem very 'sympathetic' to me.

We all react to challenges differently. At eight, I took the approach that I had to make a new life as a totally blind person. I rapidly learnt Braille, joined 18-year-old secretaries learning to touch type, and developed the ability to see through touch. Being blind is not frightening to me. I am used to it.

Almost one person in 30 has sight loss beyond correction with spectacles and the number is growing. Each day across Britain 100 people are told they are losing their sight. Who do you know in your church with sight loss? In a church of 100 people, there should, on average, be three or four people experiencing sight loss. Perhaps you haven't noticed them. Perhaps they aren't there.

In this chapter I shall look at what sight loss is, how it affects our church experience, and what we can do to help people with sight loss to feel part of church.

What is sight loss?

The range of sight disability runs from marginally impaired vision that affects our life and work, right the way through to total blindness. Around two million people in the UK have significant uncorrectable sight loss. Of these, 30,000 can see nothing. A further two million people have transitional sight loss and are awaiting correction surgery or proper spectacles.

A person's sight loss can vary depending on the time of day, the lighting and their health. Nick gets up in the morning unable to see anything. His sight gradually improves through the day. In the evening he folds up his cane and drives to church.

Are you shocked? Many people with sight loss are misjudged and accused of being frauds. Think! Have you ever walked from bright sunlight into a dark church? What could you see? Your eyes take time to adjust. Sight loss conditions can affect that transition speed, create a fog in front of the eye, or leave only a tiny tunnel to see through. If you want to understand more about sight loss conditions, see the resources at the end of the chapter.

Each person has an individual set of issues associated with their sight loss. Technology and a guide dog mean that my issues are quite different from those of Nick, who uses his constantly varying sight to cope with his situation.

In my view, the underlying framework for understanding the issues of sight loss is communication. I shall look at the way we communicate with people with sight loss in three areas: printed materials and information, places and people. I shall look at each area as it affects church, providing solutions as we go along.

First and foremost, people with sight loss are still people—not a collection of issues and sight problems. Each of us is special, made in the image of God. This understanding should govern our attitude and the way we approach the functional adjustments I discuss.

Printed materials and information

Churches are full of information. In the past, I would be handed a bundle of thick books and printed sheets. Today the information is often projected electronically on to screens or delivered via internet websites. If you can't see it, this information passes you by.

'The party was great, Mike. Why didn't you come?' Disappointedly I reply, 'I didn't know there was a party.'

'Well, you should read the notices.'

I often wish I could, but so often notices are not read out but are printed or displayed on screens.

An important part of worship is singing. Have you heard this song? 'A skyscraper to our God the rock!' Kay sang it out

lustily. Totally blind, she had never seen the words, which are in fact 'Ascribe greatness to our God the rock'.

I am technologically able, and receive notices, orders of service and songs by email. Kay enjoyed having the songs read to her, and many benefit from audio recordings of the words. Modified print is easy to create with a word processor. Try putting out large-print copies of songs and church materials in bold sans-serif 17-point print. You will be amazed at how many people take them.

At the Keswick Convention, Joan (94), who lost her sight last year through macular degeneration, asked me if she could learn Braille. 'I can't see the letters now. They all just jump around.' I gave her the songs in giant 25-point print. Joan came back at the end of the meeting beaming. 'These letters don't jump! It's wonderful. I've so enjoyed singing the songs tonight. It's been wonderful to join in the worship with everyone else.'

Joining together in spoken parts of a service can be very inclusive. One night, at the big top in Spring Harvest, we tried an experimental liturgy. Half the congregation were blindfolded. I asked everyone to join me in saying the words together. The feedback from the blindfolded folk was that they felt excluded and isolated, as if they didn't belong. How many feel that way in our churches? Since then, Torch Trust has started producing Braille and large/giant printouts with the words on the screen for each evening celebration during certain weeks of Spring Harvest. Ken, a Braille reader, said, 'I'm part of it now… I've been able to join with everyone else. It's been absolutely fantastic.'

Action songs can be great fun, but there are so many, and they all have a lot of different movements. If you can see, it is much easier to join in. After nearly felling someone by stamping my foot when I was supposed to be taking their hand, I tend not to join in these days. That's an aspect of inclusion I have rather given up on.

PowerPoint has kept many a wandering preacher on track, but make sure that there are no points that are only conveyed visually. Give a verbal description for those who can't see.

Most of us get information over the web. This is true for people with sight loss as well. Does your church website conform to access standards? So many church websites are carelessly built. My talking screenreader just splutters out incomprehensible sets of numbers and letters. For advice, see the link at the end of this chapter.

The Bible is central to the Christian experience. Standard-print Bibles are now supplemented by many other formats. I use the Bible on the internet, have it in my phone and possess some ebook Bibles, together with spoken voice recordings on my MP3 players. Torch Trust has a webpage listing Bible resources that include giant print, Braille, and even special pocket-sized audio Bibles. God's word can be very accessible today.

Places

Getting to church can be quite a challenge. I can't see the spires or signs, and public transport is virtually non-existent on Sundays. An offer of consistent transport to church can make the difference, for someone with sight loss, between attending or staying at home. A team approach can be useful, but make sure that the person knows exactly who is coming.

First impressions are vital. I moved house and decided to try a good church I had heard about. My guide dog managed to find the church. As I entered, I called out, 'Hello!' People were chatting and there was an uninterested responding grunt.

'Where shall I go?' I asked.

'Over there,' someone said. I think they were pointing.

My dog found his way to a seat in the church, and, just before the service started, someone sat next to me. 'That's nice,' I said, 'to have someone from the church sit next to me.'

'I'm a visitor,' he replied. That was not the right church for me.

In contrast, I walked into a north Birmingham church and was greeted with 'Hello, gorgeous, would you like a drink?' Though flattered, I was not the 'gorgeous' one, and my dog got the drink. However, that church had Braille songs and a place for my dog to sleep out the service, and someone helped me with the coffee and meeting people. That's the sort of welcome that makes you want to come back.

The phone call was a strange one: 'Should we put orange dayglo strips around the pillars in our church?' Well, most people want to hide those pillars. Apparently, the church was so gloomy that people were injuring themselves against the solid stone pillars. Orange strips would be ghastly. Think about what your church looks like, especially for those who don't see too well. I suggested some bright pictures and a not-too-distant makeover.

Often, people with sight loss will need help around the church or at events and house groups. Don't go behind and push. We feel safer if you go ahead and allow us to take your arm. We will then feel where you are going and will be able to tell if you are going up or down steps. Torch Trust has advice on sighted guiding (see the links at the end of this chapter).

- Lighting should be even. Partially sighted Robert tells me he is often bumping into people as he moves from one pool of light to another.
- Make sure steps are clearly visible, with contrasting colours.

- Can a person with sight loss find their way into the next room? We went to a very modern church where everything was in a contemporary red. Even the door handles were difficult to spot. Door frames, doors and handles should be in contrasting colours.
- Don't forget to clear out the clutter. Not only is it a fire hazard, but it can block the way for pushchairs and trip up those who can't see well.

Does someone need help? Don't assume you know what help they will need. I was giving computer training to a blind man who came in spitting tacks.

'You won't learn anything if you carry on like that,' I said.

'You would be angry if you'd just had the experience I've had. I've been crossed across a road I didn't want to cross. And I'm very cross!'

That evening I waited at the crossing outside the centre. When someone helped me over the road, I thanked him politely.

'You're a lot more pleasant than the blind idiot I 'elped this morning,' I heard. This crossing helper must hover there all day!

Jesus always asked people what help they needed. Talking to Bartimaeus, he asked, 'What do you want me to do for you?' (Mark 10:51, NIV). Let's follow Jesus' example.

People

The Royal National Institute of Blind People carried out a survey to discover the real issues faced by people with sight loss. I thought the answer would be something to do with reading or getting around, but it turned out to be 'social isolation'.

Vic, who lost his sight overnight, cut himself off from everything because he was so frightened. If you can't see well, you can't make contact and communicate with people very easily. The only way you will catch my eye is if I throw it to you: it's made of plastic!

A lot of church fellowship takes place in crowded coffee rooms. My best friend could be standing just feet away and I would have no idea they were there. Much communication takes place through gesture and other non-verbal means. We are often seen as rather unfriendly. We often find it hard to locate people and initiate conversations, so we tend to respond to those who communicate with us. I am pretty proactive and outgoing, and I can compensate for this, but people with sight loss are a cross-section of personality types. The quieter ones unthinkingly get left out. Speaking on Torch Trust's *Foursight for the Church* DVD, Sheila, who is blind, says that 'just to be accepted as a part of the body, as a person, is so important—it makes all the difference in the world'.

Don't group disabled people together in special areas of the church or tables at meals. I call these 'crips corners'. Even blind people don't necessarily share much in common. How would you like to be placed in a special group just because you are losing your hair?

Touch is an important aspect of communication. The rather reticent British find this difficult, but for folk with sight loss, touch can be useful. You can politely indicate by touch that you are talking to someone, and you will certainly need to touch if you are to guide people and help with tasks.

Do talk. I know that it may be a challenge to get started, especially without eye contact. Some partially sighted people will look at you sideways because that's the only way they can see you. Don't struggle for words. Just use words that come naturally. 'Did you watch that programme last night? Do you want to see the house group leader?' These are fine. Don't worry about using words like 'blind' or 'visually impaired', but try to listen and use the words a disabled person uses.

Language can be a stumbling block in presenting biblical truth. Blindness is often used as a picture of unbelief, and light is a very strong Christian concept. How can we explain those ideas to someone who has never seen? In groups, I often run a test. 'How do you explain the colour red to someone who has never seen?' Answers include, 'Red is hot, an indication of danger, a stop traffic light.' I then ask, 'Who is wearing red?' (There's always someone.) 'Stop her! She's hot and dangerous!'

Please include non-visual elements in explanations of Christian truth. These can complement those amazing visuals that are lost on me and others with sight loss.

Christian fellowship in a loving church can overcome the huge issue of 'social isolation' that is experienced by so many blind, partially sighted and other disabled people. Torch Trust can work with churches to start local fellowship groups specifically designed to reach out to people with sight loss in the local community.

A missional opportunity: the sight loss journey

God is challenging us at Torch Trust to help the hundred people who are losing their sight each day. The journey usually starts at an eye clinic when someone is told, 'I am afraid there is nothing that can be done about your sight loss.'

Torch Trust is planning to recruit and train volunteers in churches, especially those near eye clinics. The volunteers will come alongside people losing their sight, as Christian friends, complementing the support provided by hard-pressed health and social care professionals and bringing the love of Jesus into their challenging situation. Perhaps you and your church would like to share in this voluntary activity.

Resources

Register your church with Foursight for the Church at www. torch-foursight.org to receive a free church pack and access to online resources.

In the Foursight church pack is a booklet called *A Clearer Vision*, which contains guidance for making church more accessible to people with sight loss, including a brief introduction to sighted guiding. Leaflets about awareness training and accessible resources for churches are also included.

- For help in preparing accessible worship resources, go to www.torchtrust.org/smartweb/foursight/accessibleworship
- To find Bibles in accessible formats, go to www.torchtrust.org/bibles
- To learn more about Torch groups, go to www.torchtrust.org/smartweb/groups-and-fellowship
- For guidance on making websites accessible, go to www.rnib.org.uk/professionals/webaccessibility/pages

Chapter 11
Including people with hearing loss

This chapter was written mainly by Tracy Williamson, with a section by Gill Behenna on including deaf people, and signing.

Deafness

Noise jangling
A muddle of sound
Voices passing to and fro
I smile, trying to look as if I know
What is going on.
A joke
Shrill laughter
Helpless hilarity
I laugh, trying to prove to myself
That I belong.
Why do I try?
Why do I never express the cry
That echoes in my heart
As in the laughing, talking group
I sit, cut off
A person apart?

I wrote this poem while I was with a group of friends. I loved that they were having fun, but the more laughs they shared, the more isolated I felt. I started jotting down phrases about how it felt and the poem came into being. Everyone's experience of deafness is different, but most will identify with the feeling of isolation I experienced then, and still often do.

Ruth smiled at the woman hesitantly approaching the church. 'Hello,' she said, 'Welcome to the service. I'm Ruth. What is your name?'

'No, I've never been before,' Sheila replied, and then, as Ruth looked puzzled, hurriedly interjected, 'Oh, I'm sorry, I thought you said, "It's nice to see you here again"!'

Embarrassed, Sheila quickly found a seat apart from the other worshippers. They were chatting happily together as they waited for the service to begin, and she shifted nervously, hoping that no one would try to talk to her.

Two hours later, Sheila was home again. Frustration filled her as she reviewed her morning—that first embarrassing mistake, followed by the notices, singing, sermon and fellowship time at the end. They'd been inspiring to everyone else, perhaps, but quite meaningless to her. 'It's useless,' she thought, 'I'll never manage to be part of church. I won't bother trying again.'

This has been the typical experience of many people who, because of their hearing loss, find it a struggle to be part of church. One in every seven people in Great Britain suffers from some degree of hearing loss. This chapter looks at how our churches can become places where people with hearing impairment, as much as any other people group, are truly included.

The key issue: isolation

People often associate deafness with living in a silent world. For many deaf/Deaf people, that is truly the case, but equally hard is the struggle faced by those with a partial loss. You feel completely isolated when you can hear all the sounds around you but not well enough to understand them, when you can hear people talking but not what they say. The sounds of everyday life are a discordant muddle.

Communication forms the heart of church life—communication between minister and congregation, between individual members, and with the outside community. Whatever denomination, size or style of church you attend, its aim is to worship and serve God through singing, Bible reading, preaching, listening and responding, giving, serving, caring, enjoying fellowship, teaching Sunday school or reaching out into our communities. The essence of all this is communication.

If your hearing is impaired, all of these areas of church life are affected. Instead of being a safe place of trust, growth, love and mutual respect, church can become a source of pain and isolation.

Don, the Chair of Open Ears, a Christian charity for people who are hard of hearing, is severely deafened:

Never being sure whether one has heard correctly (even when one has) makes for a continuous attitude of hesitancy and uncertainty, for fear of saying something inappropriate, or something which has already been said by someone else, and therefore looking stupid. A general feeling of being 'out of control' colours one's attitude to life. This can lead to social withdrawal into a 'safe' place.

Terminology

Deafness and hearing loss are umbrella terms covering a wide range of degrees and types of loss, from the very slight to the profound. The effects are as varied as the people themselves. The following are the most likely terms that people will use:

- Hard of hearing (usually mild to moderate loss)
- Hearing impaired/hearing challenged (mild to severe loss)
- Partially deaf/partially hearing (moderate to severe loss)
- Deafened (hearing loss acquired through age, accident or illness)
- Deaf/severely deaf (moderate to profound loss)
- Profoundly deaf (severe to total loss)

Deaf people (with a capital D) are those who are part of the Deaf community, which has its own culture and language.

Levels of hearing loss

We use the term 'hearing loss' to cover any impairment in hearing. The quietest sounds that people with mild deafness can hear are 25–39 decibels, while the figure is 40–69 decibels for people with moderate deafness, 70–94 decibels for people who are severaly deaf and more than 95 decibels for those who are profoundly deaf (figures taken from www. actiononhearingloss.org.uk).

Hearing loss can affect people in many ways related to the fact that they are not hearing as others do. Psychological effects may include:

- Isolation and loneliness; feeling left out; a reduced circle of friends.
- Embarrassment from misunderstandings. This can result in social awkwardness, lack of confidence and erosion of self-esteem, and fear of engaging in social occasions.
- Frustration and confusion caused by not understanding what's being said. This can lead to stress, anger or self-pity, and even to depression.

There can be physical effects as well:

- Tiredness because of having to be on 'high alert' all the time to try to hear/understand what's going on.
- Reduced ability to speak/communicate well (for example, slurred speech or mispronunciation of words).
- Short concentration span (because of the huge amount of concentration always required to follow what is going on).

Including Deaf people

Gill Behenna, of Signs of God, writes:

A significant minority of people with a hearing loss would identify themselves as being Deaf users of British Sign Language (BSL) and belonging to the Deaf community in Britain. As you will see, Deaf people often refer to themselves using an upper case 'D' in Deaf. The language of disability or impairment would not be appropriate to use when talking with or about this group of people.

Practical issues

Many Deaf people use BSL as their first or preferred language. This means that access to mainstream churches will probably be via the use of Sign Language interpreters. In Britain at the time of writing, there is a shortage of properly trained and qualified BSL/English interpreters, and even fewer who are skilled in the knowledge of religious language, so access to mainstream worship and teaching remains difficult.

Many Deaf people prefer to attend worship that is conducted entirely in BSL so that they can access direct teaching, worship and fellowship in their own language. Some Deaf people prefer to attend a mixture of Deaf-led worship and mainstream worship. More information about including Deaf BSL users in the life of the church is available from the *Sign Me In!* policy document available from Go! Sign (see links at the end of this chapter).

For Deaf people who use BSL, it's always helpful to use as much visual material in worship as possible. The use of projected hymn words, Bible passages and liturgy is very helpful, since, for example, it frees up Deaf people's hands for sign language. It's not possible to hold a book and sign at the same time.

When interpreters are used in church services, care needs to be taken in ensuring that they have all the information they need in order to work effectively. BSL has a different structure than the English language, so the translation of liturgy, hymns and songs is a skilled and complicated task. Hymns often use metaphors that do not translate easily from one language to another without creating a new song, and this can't be done without preparation. More information about working with interpreters is available from Signs of God (see links at the end of this chapter).

Issues of language

There needs to be great sensitivity over the use of the language of healing and in the offering of prayer ministry. It should never be assumed that a Deaf person wants to become hearing and, as in any prayer ministry, people should be asked what they want prayer for. People offering prayer ministry to Deaf people should be able to sign well (at least to level 2) or make use of an interpreter to ensure that the Deaf person feels included and confident.

A Deaf person who uses BSL as their first or preferred language may regard it as a natural part of their identity. To be told that when they get to heaven they will become hearing is to suggest that their identity is flawed in some way and unacceptable to God. It would be similar to a French person being told that when they get to heaven they will become English. Instead, it's more helpful to speak about a heavenly vision of wholeness where earthly restrictions are past. After all (who knows?), maybe everyone in heaven can use sign language!

Issues of inclusion

Deaf people can gain access to the worship of a mainstream church through BSL/English interpreters, but this does not necessarily lead to their being included. Many Deaf people remain passive observers of the worship instead of becoming involved and actively participating. The challenge to any mainstream church is not simply to use interpreters for the worship but to seek ways in which Deaf people can be included and participate and grow into Christian disciples, leaders and ministers. This means inclusion in and access to house groups, social events, teaching events and the governance and leadership of the church.

There is a sense in which many Deaf people feel that their access to worship is 'second hand' when it is received through an interpreter. The congregation in one church decided to change this. They were used to having an interpreter for a small group of Deaf people who attended the morning service once a month, but felt that they should do more to include Deaf people in the church. They suggested that, instead of having the service led in English as usual, once a month it should be led in BSL by a minister who could sign. The interpreter would then provide the 'voice' for the hearing congregation; he or she would interpret into English what was being signed. In this way, once a month, the hearing majority would get a taste of having their worship 'second hand' while the Deaf congregation received the service in their own language. Many of the regular congregation look forward to worshipping in this way and have gradually come to learn some sign language.

Of course, this way of worship depends on the availability of a minister who is fluent in BSL, and there are few such ministers, but there is no reason why Deaf people cannot be included in the rota of people who read the Bible or offer intercessions. Bible readings and prayers can be offered in BSL and interpreted into English. Why not invite Deaf people to teach a song in BSL that everyone can sign?

A note on interpreters

Please remember that sign language interpreters are there to give Deaf people access to the life and worship of the church. Please don't ask them to do something that a Deaf person should do, such as teach the congregation a BSL song, or assume that the interpreter will be pastorally responsible for the Deaf people in the congregation.

Tracy Williamson shares some of the things she has found hardest about church life.

Worship

As a young Christian, I had a mild hearing loss and wore hearing aids. I could hear if there was music playing and I did join in the worship. However, if there was a band or people clapping along, I would soon lose my place, which is disconcerting if you find yourself singing loudly when everyone else has finished. Nowadays, with a severe loss, I cannot hear the music or how fast people are singing, so I usually remain silent. But help can be given very simply by someone who is willing to show me, perhaps by pointing to the words each time we start a new verse. It is this kind of simple gesture that can help a deaf person feel much more included.

Speech and prayers

Using a PA system always helps, especially if there is a loop fitted (more about loops later). The worst thing is when people share a testimony or pray from within the congregation, unamplified. I don't even know they're speaking.

Many people think that hearing aids correct the loss, and that is all the help necessary, but hearing aids amplify every sound in the vicinity, causing a constant clamour to bombard the wearer. The sound of rustling sweet wrappers, pages flicking over, passing traffic or scraping chairs often obscures the sound of the voice that the person is trying desperately to hear.

My hearing has deteriorated and I am now severely deaf. I cannot lip-read as I am also partially sighted, so, without interpretation, it is as if I am in a foreign land with no knowledge of the language at all.

Times of fellowship

Church social situations are especially nerve-racking because the deaf person, like everyone else, wants to be part of the family, able to encourage those who are struggling or to laugh with others who are sharing a funny story. House groups and small church prayer groups can also be very isolating as a loop is often available only in the main church hall, and in small groups everyone tends to talk at once or mutter their prayers into their chests.

What can be done?

- Ask the hearing-impaired person what will be helpful to them. It sounds simple and obvious, but most of the time it never happens.

- It's helpful to me if someone types what is being said into a laptop or iPad. If the meeting is long, more than one person may need to share the task.
- Many people find it helpful for someone to take notes during the sermon or the meeting, going through them together afterwards.

The best way to find out is to ask. Some people with hearing loss may be shy about asking you, so take the initiative and ask them.

Induction loop systems

A loop is a special amplification system that transmits from the PA unit direct to people's hearing aids. Loops are a wonderful and vital help to hearing aid users: a fact sheet is available from Open Ears (see links at end of chapter). Installing the loop in itself is easy, but consideration is needed as to what loop will suit the building and the needs of the people, as there are different loops for different situations. A small portable loop can be used for a prayer or Bible study group, for example, with the microphone being passed from person to person. Be sure to advertise that your church has a loop, with notices at the entrance, in the loop area and on your website.

Church lighting

A hearing-impaired person relies on being able to see clearly. Even I, who cannot lip-read, feel completely lost if I cannot see people's faces, so speakers should stand where they are most easily seen. Good overhead lighting is essential. It can be a serious distraction if the speaker moves around a lot while talking. You may hear the plea, 'Stand still!'

Church notices and service information

Clear projection of hymn words, notices, readings and prayers is very helpful. When inviting people to join in prayers or liturgy from the screen, give them time to find the place before beginning.

Other points to consider

- BSL signers may need a platform so that they can be clearly seen.
- Consider providing 'lip-speakers' for people who are lip-readers. More information about this is available from SilentSounds (see links at end of chapter).
- Speech-to-text interpretation (STT) is generally used in larger venues. This displays a projection of the talk as it happens, and requires a skilled operator.

Resources

Go! Sign
Friendship House
484 Southchurch Road
Southend on Sea
SS1 2QA
www.deafchristian.org.uk

This is a UK-based charity committed to helping Deaf people to come to know Christ, accept him as their Saviour and grow in him. Go! Sign supports deaf and hearing signers and encourages every local church (deaf and mainstream) to provide better access to church life.

Signs of God
1 Saxon Way
Bradley Stoke
Bristol
BS32 9AR
www.signsofgod.org.uk
email: info@signsofgod.org.uk

Signs of God encourages people to develop and improve their use of BSL in Christian settings.

Open Ears
www.openears.org.uk

Open Ears (formerly The Hard of Hearing Christian Fellowship) is a charity that seeks to bring regular fellowship and prayer support to hard of hearing, deafened and deaf Christians, and deaf awareness to churches.

Action on Hearing Loss
www.actiononhearingloss.org.uk

Action on Hearing Loss (formerly RNID) produces information about induction loops and other aids for hearing-impaired people.

Silent Sounds
www.silent-sounds.co.uk

Silent Sounds promotes deaf awareness and provides services for the deaf community.

Thanks to the Diocese of Guildford for information obtained through their pamphlet *Deaf Awareness: Including D/deaf people in the life of the church*, by Susan Bloomfield © 2007.

Chapter 12
Including people with mobility difficulty

This chapter was written by Tim Wood, Chief Executive of Through the Roof. Tim has 20 years' experience of working on local, national and international projects to enable the full inclusion of disabled people in education, sport, community and church life.

'Assume nothing—always ask' was the mantra of Paul Dicken, founder of Christian disability charity Through the Roof (www. throughtheroof.org). It is a wise and relevant attitude to adopt when interacting with anyone, particularly those with mobility and/or other difficulties, who are often ignored, marginalised and misunderstood.

In the same way that each one of us is an individual, uniquely made in God's image, no two people with mobility difficulties are the same. Restrictions of mobility come in many different guises. Some people are disabled from birth through conditions such as cerebral palsy and muscular dystrophy, while others acquire disability through road traffic accidents, workplace incidents or age-related conditions such as osteoporosis or decreased strength and flexibility.

It may appear obvious, but it is important that each of us relates to a disabled individual directly by asking a question or offering support, not assuming what can or can't be done because of someone's physical appearance.

This chapter first highlights a key issue for those with mobility difficulties—the mindset of some people towards them. It then profiles three real-life experiences: two church members with mobility difficulties (one congenital, one acquired) tell their stories, then one church witnesses to the blessings it has received through venturing into disability ministry. The chapter concludes with a helpful checklist of considerations related to issues of mobility, and signposts to further help and resources.

The key issue: more than just a ramp

Often the first instinct when faced with a person with restricted mobility is to visualise the provision of ramped access into a church building that has steps. However, the biggest issue is not about ramps. I would suggest it is the restricted thinking that many people have towards disabled people.

Now Jesus met many people with illnesses and disabilities, but I don't believe Jesus ever saw a 'disabled person'; he saw a person, a full and whole person, who may have had a disability but had much more to him or her than that… [Jesus] revealed there were many around who were far more disabled, paralysed by legalism and having suffered an amputation of compassion and care.
NICK STANYON, FROM WWW.THROUGHTHEROOF.ORG/FULL-HUMANITY

Imagine what it would be like if people always focused on what you couldn't do or, worse still, what they *perceived* you couldn't do. Initially frustrating and annoying, if these approaches continued over months and years they would become self-fulfilling prophecies and destructive influences, quashing any potential hope of what could 'be' in your life. That is what many disabled people face on a daily basis.

Well-known Christian speaker and author Jeff Lucas spent time in a wheelchair and on crutches after having torn a leg muscle. 'I suddenly realised the indignity that disabled people experience,' he said, describing how people talked over him rather than to him. 'How tragic when it happens in the life of the church.'

We can easily fall into two opposing traps. Either the person who is limited in mobility is ignored completely and their needs are not considered, or others overcompensate for their impairment and they are 'wrapped in cotton wool', with an assumption that they are unable to do anything. Both approaches are unhelpful and ignore the equal value of a fellow human being created in God's image. They also disempower the person concerned, leaving them as a spectator to proceedings, often causing a negative impact on them.

Although mobility difficulties do pose some limitations, they don't necessarily extend to people's intellectual ability or their capacity to understand, talk and contribute to church and community life.

See the person, not the disability

Andrew Bartley is active in his local church and community and uses a mobility scooter to get around, having been born with Muscular Dystrophy. He gives his perspective on 'accessible church'.

As far as I am concerned, an accessible church is one where the members 'ignore' the disability and 'see' or relate to the disabled person.

My experience of the church I attend is that it feels as if my disability is not there, which is much preferable to having it highlighted all the time. It isn't that people are afraid to ask me about my condition, but it's just not an issue, and I'm able to ask for help or make suggestions about things that would be of use.

Getting a balance is difficult between over-attention and total lack of acknowledgment. I need 'attention' when there is a need, such as arranging an event or planning a building project. It is helpful if people envisage what is needed to make life easier for me and other disabled people, which often comes down to common sense.

I was once invited to speak on disability awareness at an event which was upstairs. As I use a mobility scooter to get around and can't climb steps or stairs, the meeting was quickly rearranged to a downstairs meeting room. As responsibility is on both parties, this could have been prevented with a little thought and communication, and I could have asked the question about the venue when making plans to speak there.

I like it when I am asked if I need help, but, even if it is very obvious that I need help, I may choose to refuse help and struggle on. However, please do not refuse me if I eat humble pie and come back to you to ask for help after declining it previously. If we all considered one another, with more respect for people who are different, life would be a whole lot better for everyone.

Temporarily non-disabled

We could all be said to be temporarily non-disabled, as 95 per cent of us will experience disability at some point in our lives. Heather Lewis is an active member of her church's leadership and worship teams and became temporarily immobile through a gardening accident. She reflects on her experience.

I broke my ankle recently and, over the course of four months, graduated through six plaster casts and a cumbersome boot to walking with crutches.

There was a lot to cope with from day to day, apart from the actual injury. Planning what was possible, prioritising the use of energy and making sure things were within reach when I was immobile were all challenges to face. I'm used to doing everything, so it was important to let other people 'have a turn'.

Dependence on others didn't come easily but, if you are physically immobile, you can still offer advice, reminders and suggestions. Having people who offered help, and listened to what I thought would make life easier, helped me to maintain some measure of control over my life. Small achievements can have a big impact on morale, so something simple will often enable someone to continue to participate in normal activities.

When I first ventured out, it was in a wheelchair, as my only alternative was a walking frame. I guess, like most people, I care what people think, and a walking frame doesn't go with the image I want to leave with anyone, whether they're people I know or strangers. On a practical level, I felt very vulnerable and a wheelchair offered a measure of protection and made my disability very obvious. Being able to relax and not worry about whether I would be marooned with nowhere to sit down, or whether someone might bump into me, enabled me to participate in what was happening, join in conversations and also carry things. Using all one's energy and limbs to mobilise leaves little facility to pick up or carry things.

Similarly, as I become more mobile, I am using crutches, especially in public places, to highlight the fact that my mobility is limited and to minimise the fear of falling, as people may expect that I can move faster than is yet possible.

I would prefer someone to offer help, saying something

111

like 'Shall I find you a chair?' or 'Can I carry that for you?' as it is a gesture of kindness for which I may be very grateful. Alternatively, I can decline the offer with thanks and feel that I'm not doing so badly. I really appreciate the encouragement I have received. The fact that people notice an improvement from week to week highlights progress that, from day to day, seems very small. It is also encouraging if other people suggest things that you may be able to resume doing, even if their timing isn't quite right.

It is more blessed to give than to receive

Reaching out to, and providing for, those with mobility and/or other difficulties not only assists the disabled individual but also the whole community of believers, as described here by a member of Crossways Community Baptist Church, Dorking.

The church is blessed because everyone taking part receives back far, far more than they give, and all have grown in faith as a result.

Having been convicted by the Lord in July 2004 of the need for a ministry designed to bring support to those individuals in the community with spiritual, mental, social or physical problems, after much prayer 'Project 61' began. It was an umbrella organisation, able to respond to needs as they arose, and taking as its commission Isaiah 61:1–3. As time has gone on, it has become apparent that this is so much a reflection of the church that we now consider it to be our community ministry and are no longer calling it 'Project 61'. We have also rewritten our vision statement as follows: 'Our vision is to be an inclusive church that encourages all to grow into relationship with God and presents Jesus in a way that all people can understand and respond to.'

The church was built in 1876 with a variety of different floor levels, so it was not built with disabilities in mind. Because of this, we have carried out a number of alterations to the building, putting in new, wider exterior doors and ramps and changing floor levels, all of which has made the majority of the building accessible to all. We also have an easy-access toilet designed with wheelchair users in mind, with facilities to cover all toiletry needs including support rails, disposable gloves and disinfectant wipes. We will continue to adjust and adapt as needs arise.

Inclusivity checklist

Many churches have undertaken refurbishment or adaptation of their building facilities and activities to enable the greater inclusivity and access of those with mobility difficulties. The following checklist highlights some key considerations:

- Welcome and be open to disabled people to create a sense of 'belonging'.
- Focus on what someone can do rather than what they can't, and ensure that they have opportunities to use their God-given talents to contribute to church life.
- Speak directly to disabled people, assuming nothing and asking them how they can best be supported and included.
- When talking with a wheelchair user, they will appreciate it if you can be on the same level as them.
- Don't lean on, move or push a wheelchair without the user's permission: it is part of their personal space.
- Offer reserved parking and drop-off points at your church venue.
- Have 'step-free' access giving level/ramped entry to buildings.
- Any ramps or steps should have a handrail.

- Provide accessible toilets.
- Offer seating (some with arms) near the entrance/exit.
- Ensure that your website is accessible and has relevant information about facilities that help disabled people access the building and activities.

Further resources

The following three publications offer advice on how to assist people with mobility and/or other difficulties in a church context.

- *Come In*: a guide to making church buildings and their environment accessible for disabled people
- *Removing Barriers*: a self-assessment questionnaire to assess how inclusive your church activities and facilities are for disabled people
- *Be a Roofbreaker: Equipping churches to become welcoming places for all*: this publication contains sections on the inclusion of wheelchair users and those with mobility difficulties as well as many other disabilities.

These resources are published by Through the Roof and are available at www.throughtheroof.org/shop. Through the Roof also offers other written publications, training and online ideas and resources to equip churches and Christians on their journey towards greater inclusion of disabled people. Contact 01372 749955; info@throughtheroof.org; www.throughtheroof.org; www.facebook.com/throughtheroof

- The Outlook Trust is a Christian charity that reaches out to older people, many of whom will struggle with the same issues as people with mobility difficulties: www.outlook-trust.org.uk

- The National Churches Trust promotes and supports church buildings as places of historic, architectural and community value. It is a source of support, advice and potential grants to churches making changes: www.nationalchurchestrust.org

- Churches may wish to arrange an access audit of their premises. Contact the National Register of Access Consultants, an independent register of accredited Access Auditors and Consultants: www.nrac.org.uk

Chapter 13

Including people with mental health conditions

This chapter was written by Jonathan Clark, Director for Premier Life at Premier Christian Media. He is responsible for Premier Lifeline—Confidential Christian Helpline; Premier Mind and Soul—Christian Response to Mental Health; Healing and Wholeness; and Premier's Prayer Team. He has worked in the field of mental health since 1983.

If I were to ask whether Christians experience problems with their physical health, almost everyone would say 'yes'. If I ask the same question about mental health, however, people will often be more reticent, sometimes even answering 'no' when the real answer is 'yes'. This is strange, as the range of types and causes of mental health problems is just as varied and complex as is found with physical health.

Here's another puzzle. If people go to their GP or hospital consultant about their physical health and are given medication, it is normal for them to take it. However, I frequently hear people ask or be asked whether they should take the medication for their mental health that has been prescribed by a doctor or consultant. It is as if there is something very different about mental health.

When a person has a physical illness or long-term physical condition, it is seen as a normal occurrence and consequently it is expected that they will seek treatment. So why, when that same person has a mental illness, would they be told not to seek help or take medication, and be seen as a failure by others or even themselves? We do not need to hold seminars based on the question 'Should Christians take insulin if they're diabetic?' so why should we have seminars entitled 'Should Christians take anti-depressants?'

Many disabilities are physical and can be recognised because they are visible. Others are less obvious. Mental health problems are not physically visible because they affect the mind, thoughts, emotions and behaviour. Yet the range of conditions covered by mental health is as broad and deep as that of physical health, so the occurrence of mental illness is likely to be as common as physical illness. The statistics are as follows: one in four adults in the United Kingdom experiences at least one diagnosable mental health problem in any one year, and one in six is experiencing mental health problems at any given time (Office for National Statistics: *Psychiatric Morbidity Report*, 2001). In the same way, mental illnesses vary in degree from mild to severe and in duration from short-term to enduring.

The culture in parts of the church of denying or undermining the treatment of mental health conditions can be just as dangerous as challenging the medical diagnosis for a serious physical illness. Over the years, many people have struggled with mental health issues privately, not telling anyone at church what they are going through for fear that, if they do, they will be criticised, condemned, misconstrued or rejected. Many have been told, 'Pull yourself together', 'Repent of the sin of self-pity', 'Count your blessings', 'Stop lacking faith' or 'What you need is deliverance', when all they have really needed from the church is a listening ear, acceptance, encouragement and support—in fact, a bit of love in action.

One of the key aspects of mental illness is that, by and large, it starts to impact people during their life, as opposed to being something they are born with and have to adapt to from their earliest years. For some, it may develop in childhood, but for others it could begin in adolescence or early adult life. Others still will develop mental health problems at varying stages of adulthood or in senior years. Anyone has the potential to experience mental health problems. Mental illness is something that affects often otherwise healthy individuals and can strike at any age.

Schizophrenia, a particularly disturbing condition that may include symptoms of thought disorder, hallucinations, paranoia and delusions, is often first experienced when a person is in their teens or 20s. Up to that age, the individual may have had a normal childhood, with all the usual expectations for their future including school, college, career and relationships, but at some point they begin to experience disordered thoughts and their life changes direction. Their sense of loss can be great, along with their family's, when they realise the impact of the condition on their life.

Some conditions creep up and take a person unawares; others can have quite a sudden onset. They can be triggered by stress, pressure, illness, medication, drug use, relationship breakdown, hormonal changes and a whole range of other factors. Some may be the result of choices such as alcohol and drug use. Others will be due to unexpected life events such as experiencing trauma or the death of a loved one.

Imagine a person with a career, full of hopes and dreams for the future, suddenly hit by a mental health problem. It may be schizophrenia, but could just as easily be bipolar disorder, depression, post-traumatic stress disorder or borderline personality disorder. Work becomes impossible, life goes into turmoil, thoughts and feelings are in disarray, and hopes and dreams go out of the window. Little wonder some people lose hope and consider suicide. Living with a mental illness is a challenge to the individual and they have to come to terms with the changes (if they are even able to recognise that they are ill); it is also a challenge to everyone around them, including church members.

How does the church respond to someone who is suffering from a mental illness?

Identifying someone's mental ill-health can be the initial challenge: recognising the change in a person who has been in the church for years—the change in their personality, behaviour, speech, interests, activities or involvement. This change can show in the form of withdrawal but also in either over-involvement or over-demanding behaviours, depending on the condition. Some will develop bizarre behaviours, which are more obvious.

In the English language there are a host of words that relate to mental disorder, many of which are slang and colloquial words. Why so many? Probably because the disorder of the mind in one person challenges the people around them and creates a sense of insecurity, fear and discomfort in the observers. However, we need to recognise that the person's mental disorder does not alter their humanity. They are just as much a person who is loved by God as anyone else (especially as God looks at the heart and sees their distress). We must never forget that a person with a mental illness is first and foremost a person with needs for love, care, support, compassion, fellowship and relationships. It is important to recognise their condition and how it may affect them, but it is just as important to recognise that they are still spiritual beings and still have spiritual needs.

Differing conditions result in different needs. For example, depression may be caused by a build-up of difficult circumstances and may therefore be traced to life events; however, it can creep from the inside out. Either way, once depression has taken hold, it can be all-consuming, and you cannot simply tell people to 'snap out of it'. People in the depths of depression may experience being in a confined dark place or pit. They may feel as if walls are closing in on them. They can feel isolated and alone. It can seem as if a dark cloud has enveloped them, or that they are in an endless tunnel with no sign of light. Even if they are Christians, they can feel totally alone. They feel 'cast... into the lowest depth', as the famous preacher Charles Spurgeon described it in his talk 'When a Preacher is Downcast', 'knowing by most painful experience what deep depression of spirit means'.

King David, when he wrote Psalm 23, said, 'Even though I walk through the valley of the shadow of death, I will fear no evil, for you are with me; your rod and your staff, they comfort me' (Psalm 23:4). Suffering from depression can feel like going through the valley of the shadow of death: the mountains may tower on either side; it may feel as if all is closing in. There is a need for support, care and help. We know that God is there but we may not see or feel him. At times like these, there is a need to hold on to the promises of God and trust that, as we reach out to him, he will hold us up.

In Psalm 40, David recalls, 'I waited patiently for the Lord; he turned to me and heard my cry. He lifted me out of the slimy pit, out of the mud and mire; he set my feet on a rock and gave me a firm place to stand' (vv. 1–2). Suffering from depression can feel like the slimy pit, the mud, the mire, the place of distress, despair and despondency. It is only once we have travelled through it that we can look back and see God lifting us out.

A mental health condition that impacts all churches sooner or later is dementia, when a person who has been active all their life in church will begin to find it harder to cope with services and activities, due to memory loss and disorientation. They still have spiritual needs and, even with dementia and significant memory impairment, they can respond to Bible stories and well-known hymns, songs and choruses.

If a person is on medication, do not dissuade them from taking it. This is unethical and potentially very dangerous. They have been prescribed the medication for a reason by a qualified health professional. The person may not feel they need to take it or that it is having any effect, and you may agree with them; however, it may well be keeping them mentally stable, and you will know this only after they have stopped and they suffer a relapse in their mental health. Stopping medication suddenly can have significant adverse effects, especially if it is the type of medication that requires a planned reduction programme. If you or the person taking the medication question its appropriateness, the way forward is to ask for a reassessment by the doctor prescribing the drugs, and, if necessary, a second opinion.

It is important for the church family to be there for individuals with mental health needs, not to make demands but to support. Some may need practical help, others emotional support. Sometimes just 'being there' is what is needed.

For some, their mental health problems are temporary and they come out the other side. For others, these problems can be life-changing and longer-lasting, and the church needs to plan a course of action and support for such individuals. If there are a number of people in the church with mental health problems, each will have their own particular needs. There may be activities that can be arranged collectively, but the needs may be very different. Some people will cope well with services; others will not. Some may cope with small groups, others with larger gatherings; others still may need one-to-one interaction. For some, an informal, regular drop-in meeting place is important.

Do not be a 'Pollyanna church' where, in the words of Adrian Plass, 'everyone is so neurotically positive that nothing negative can be admitted' (Association of Christian Counsellors summer school, 2012). The challenge is to listen to God, treat everyone as a unique individual loved by God, and ask for wisdom to meet their needs. Ask God to show you how he sees the person and what his heart is for them. Accept them with unconditional love in the same way that he has accepted you and me.

Do not become transfixed by the diagnosis or label: remember that this is a person first. Offer them the church as a welcoming place of safety where they can be handled with great care and treated as a precious gift from God. Do not focus on 'fixing' individuals with mental health needs. However, do not be afraid to offer prayer. Prayer ministry and counselling can be of great benefit to people. God is still God, and can and does heal mental health problems as much as physical health problems. However, in the same way that not every person is healed physically when we pray for them, nor are they always healed mentally or psychologically when we pray. However, this should not stop us praying and bringing them into the presence of God, for the Father to touch them in whatever way he chooses.

Case studies from churches

Example 1

A small church has a residential home for people recovering from mental illness in its catchment area. One Sunday, one of the residents arrives at the service. He does not seem quite the church member they are familiar with but it is hard to define why. His clothes are not fashionable; he is a bit dishevelled; he is smoking roll-ups. He comes into the service but pops out halfway through to have a cigarette. Everyone is welcoming but slightly surprised by him.

The next week, he comes with a friend. Over the coming weeks, a number of the residents attend the services. Some are restless and many pop out for cigarette breaks. The preacher's rhetorical questions get answered! One resident is very quiet and almost withdrawn, while another is hyper and incorrigible.

All in all, the church services are never the same again. The first person felt a welcome and found a mental health-friendly church where he felt accepted. He told his friends and they came along. Over time, a number of them make decisions to follow Jesus and ask for baptism. They have found a spiritual home.

Example 2

A community care project is set up in an area where the churches have buildings that they can offer for use, but the care resources are sparse and stretched. A worker is employed to establish community resources offered jointly by the churches to their communities. Most of the churches sign up to take part and volunteers are recruited and trained. Drop-in coffee mornings/meeting places are established in each community, staffed by trained volunteers, where people can feel safe and welcomed and find a listening ear. These are also places where they might meet their key worker informally outside their home environment. Additional services established include carer support groups, adult literacy sessions, and ministers' and professionals' lunch meetings, with speakers and a chance to break down barriers.

Example 3

A church is sited opposite a residential home for people with dementia. The residents are not in a position to come to church easily, but the church has a history of holding carol services in a range of sheltered housing units, and the decision is made to offer visits to the residential home, where a group from the church will take low-key services. Most of the services are based on seasonal festivals and the hymns and readings are traditional and well known. Other services include 'songs of praise' or family favourites.

The services are carefully crafted. Readings and the talk are kept short, to the point and memorable, with illustrations when relevant. Hymns relate to the residents' school or church days and only the best-known verses are sung. The service is short and succinct but designed to feed people's spirits and enable them to sing along with hymns and choruses as the music triggers memories.

Example 4

Many churches become involved in outreach to homeless people through soup kitchens and night shelters; the challenge is how to incorporate them into church. The concept of Café Church offers an opportunity—a place where everyone is welcome and refreshments are provided. It is as much a drop-in centre as an informal service. The worship is accessible and the talks are designed to be practical and relevant to daily living. The informality may appear to others to be unplanned, but behind the scenes there is a need for coordination and planning, to ensure that all who come are included and welcomed and feel able to fully participate in 'church'.

Useful contacts

- Premier Lifeline: Confidential Christian Helpline. Offers a listening ear and emotional and spiritual support. Open 9am to midnight daily on 0845 345 0707 or 020 7316 0808
- Premier Mind and Soul: A Christian Response to Mental Health. Website features, articles, blogs and podcasts plus conferences and monthly newsletter: www.mindandsoul. info
- Association of Christian Counsellors. Represents Christians who provide counselling and pastoral care; website includes directory of Christian Counsellors: www.acc-uk.org

Chapter 14

Including families with children with additional needs

This chapter was written by Kay Morgan-Gurr, general director of Children Worldwide. Her experience of working with children and families with additional needs spans three decades, as a nurse and a children's evangelist. As well as being a children's worker and trainer, she now also works as disability consultant to Spring Harvest and other events.

Raising a child will always come with a mix of joy and challenges. In response to that, the work done with families in our churches appears to be on the increase, and the need to work with families who have a child with additional needs is becoming a greater probability, especially when you look at the facts and figures.

- Did you know that five per cent of children under the age of 16 have a disability, and 52 per cent of their families are at risk of experiencing poverty?
- Did you know that it costs up to three times as much to raise a disabled child as it does to raise a child without disabilities?
- Did you know that caring for a disabled child carries a high

risk of causing family relationship problems? According to one study, 31 per cent of couples report some problems, and nine per cent actually separate. In addition, stress, depression and lack of sleep are commonly experienced problems for the parents and siblings of children with additional needs.

FIGURES TAKEN FROM 'CONTACT A FAMILY'

By 'family', of course, we mean all shapes of family: two parents, single parent and foster parent(s).

The key issues

When there is a child with additional needs in our children's work, it is easy just to concentrate on the child—but the whole family will be in need of consideration and care. The whole family will be going through the process of coming to terms with the reality of having a child with additional needs as well as coping with the day-to-day needs of being a family. Getting a diagnosis is often long-drawn-out, and the parents will often have to fight for every extra provision that they need to care for their child. Siblings are often overlooked or, more worryingly, expected to take on the role of either a carer or a home help. Very often, when families get to church, leaders of the children's groups ask a parent to stay with their child. This is sad, because it can be the only opportunity in a week for a husband and wife to be together and gain spiritual input.

With all that in mind, when these families attend our churches, the things that they need most are a welcome, acceptance, good communication and accessibility, and, even more important than these, to feel that they belong to a community. The issues of having a child with additional needs are not present only on a Sunday. These families will have to go home and cope with multiple challenges for the rest of the week. There is much more that a church can and should do.

Ann and Derek

Ann and Derek are married and have two children, both of whom have additional needs. Due to severe autism, their older child cannot access the midweek group and needs one-to-one care on a Sunday morning. The local school cannot cope with his needs and there are no spaces available in any special schools. This means that Ann has him at home with her, with no respite care apart from two mornings when the local school has agreed to have him, with the help of a local agency.

Ann is tired, and is still trying to weigh up the idea of a loving God against the fact that she has two children with additional needs. Her younger child often gets overlooked, both at home and at church. Her husband Derek is in denial and won't accept that his children have additional needs, thus putting even more pressure on Ann. Because getting to church is so hard, they can only make the effort every other week. For the family, what happens on a Sunday is just the tip of the iceberg.

What parents want to say to you

'My child is more than just a problem to be solved.' Children with additional needs are often seen as a problem that needs managing. Leaders are recruited to deal with a problem rather than to have a vision for that child. No matter what the additional need, these children can be achievers, have a relationship with God and be used by God. The Anns and Dereks of this world need to know that others in the church truly believe that their child is made in the image of God and precious to him. They need more than a babysitter. What they want is for the leaders to have a passion and a vision for their child. They need friends with the ability to see beyond the additional need to what God can do in and through their child.

For families on the fringes of church, it should be crystal clear that the church is a safe place with a genuine welcome, where they don't have to keep fighting or apologising for their child.

'Please don't judge my child.' Not all children with additional needs have behavioural problems, but some do. Where explosive behaviour is apparent, it is important to establish if there is a 'trigger' that can be avoided next time. Examples of behavioural problem triggers are walking into the church while the music is in full flow (arriving earlier, before the music starts, can sometimes fix this issue) or someone ruffling the hair of a child who is autistic—meant as a friendly gesture but not understood that way by the child. For one child in our church, walking in at the back door, so that he came in facing the congregation (too many people 'looking at him'), triggered a spectacular meltdown.

The misconception that behavioural problems are always due to a lack of discipline is a common one, including, and perhaps especially, in our churches. Behavioural problems can manifest in many ways. It may be that a child appears to be quiet and compliant and the assumption is made that they are 'taking it all in', but it is actually their way of showing that they cannot engage with what is going on around them.

'My child is not a project for healing ministry.' Families will be dealing with a sense of bereavement, grieving for what they were anticipating and what could have been, yet, of course, still loving their child as she or he is. They often welcome prayers for healing but also value prayers for strength, peace and grace

for them and their children. Praying for healing should be done only with parental permission, and should never take the place of good provision. Regardless of a church's position on healing, there should always be good provision.

'If we get cross or angry, it's not because we are awkward parents.' Parents of children with additional needs are often unfairly labelled as angry, difficult, manipulative… or just a total pain. These families are used to having to fight for everything and are often judged by people who don't understand. Sometimes, church feels like yet another battle to be fought. If a parent appears to be angry, bear this in mind and assure them that what you are asking or saying is in order to provide more of what they need, not to find an excuse not to care. A chat over a cup of coffee is often a very helpful thing.

'Remember my other children.' Siblings often get forgotten or are used as extra carers in the children's groups. These brothers and sisters need the freedom to be who they are, and space without their sibling, to live, learn and grow. While we celebrate the tiny achievements of their brother or sister with additional needs (which is good and right), their own achievements can go unnoticed and uncelebrated.

'Foster parents need help too'. Just because a foster parent has chosen to look after a child with additional needs, it does not mean that they can cope without help. They will need the same care as any family, as they will be facing the same battles, as well as some extra ones. It's worth noting here that foster parents are usually not at liberty to tell you everything about their child; they can only give you information that is pertinent to the care needed. Allow them to set the boundaries on this, and respect the privacy that is needed and legally required.

'Sometimes I'm just too busy to read my Bible, to pray or even tell you what I need.' When you are busy, stressed and tired, making time for personal quiet time is very difficult. Even if you do find time, trying to take in what you are reading or form coherent sentences to pray is almost impossible. It is easier to get on and do things yourself than to pick up the phone, explain what you need and then wait for someone to step up and do it.

Rebecca and Joe

Rebecca and Joe have two children. Their younger child, Abbie, has complex needs due to brain damage at birth and requires a lot of care and medical intervention. Their older child, Ben, has no medical or other additional needs. Mum has to spend a lot of time at the hospital with Abbie, and hospital appointments often make it difficult to pick Ben up from school. Because of the financial strain of having a child like Abbie, Joe has to work full-time and cannot keep taking time off to make sure Ben is cared for. Getting Abbie ready for church, with tube feeds and oxygen packs, is very difficult; if her breathing is bad, she and Rebecca cannot go.

Their church put together a support group for them—hand-picked people whose role is to see where they can help both practically and spiritually. The key provisions they have put in place are that a mum whose child is at the same school picks Ben up when necessary, someone is willing to meet and pray with Rebecca and Joe, and two people who were happy to be trained in caring for Abbie take it in turns to babysit. The babysitters cover one home group/cell group per month, to allow Rebecca and Joe to go together, plus time to go on 'parent dates' with just Ben. They also sit with Abbie when she is in hospital to allow some normality for Ben, and for Rebecca to eat proper food and catch up on sleep. The support group does much more, but those are the basics.

This level of support can be achieved only with mutual trust, friendship, training and understanding.

What to do

Caring for these families is a long-term commitment, not to be taken up and put down when time allows. It will require strong friendship, deep trust on both sides and a lot of time and energy. Every family will be different in the support they need; there won't be a 'one size fits all' solution, so good communication is vital. It is a good idea to have named people who will help to coordinate what is needed, to communicate with the family and put a care plan in place. As this group gets to know the family, it will become easier to see where help is required and to meet the need, but also to celebrate with them when good things happen.

A support group needs to include more than a couple of people, should be accountable and should have a place to go if they find themselves out of their depth. Among this group of people should be someone who can act as a mentor, to help with spiritual input and to pray with the family. Where a parent needs to be in hospital with a child long-term, this could mean taking Communion to them (along with a decent 'non hospital' coffee and a doughnut). The group could also include someone who is there just for the children, trusted by them and able to step in to babysit. If Sunday is a problem for the parents, this may help them to attend a midweek study/ cell group together instead.

If it is noticed that people in the church are misunderstanding the behaviour of a child and gossiping about it, it may be appropriate (with parental permission) for the support group to explain the situation to the church—not in a heavy-handed way, but with a few facts and figures, some anecdotal stories and a plea for prayer and understanding.

The possibilities are endless and the rewards are great. Any sacrifices that may have to be made will prove to be worthwhile.

A church's experience

A church in the Midlands is developing a ministry for families of children with profound disabilities, including both physical and intellectual disabilities. The ministry currently provides additional support for the children, either in mainstream Sunday school groups with one-to-one care or in the additional Sunday group, with a high proportion of carers to children and a tailor-made programme. There is also a Saturday monthly club for the families to attend, which is open to other families in the community.

A significant transformation has taken place in the lives of the parents through the ministry of the church. Many churches are unable to care for the types of disabilities their children have, meaning that they could have been excluded from being part of a faith community altogether. The provision of practical and emotional support, consistent prayer and commitment to deep friendship and long-term relationships, through bad times as well as good, has made all the difference in the lives of these families and their children.

The church has been blessed by the presence of these families. The congregation has accepted the challenge to look at people with disabilities with fresh eyes and has seen the joy and love that the children and their families have given to the people around them.

As we try to make the arrangements necessary to include a particular family that has a child with additional needs, we should bear in mind that it is actually about 'belonging'. We will have succeeded if the result is a family feeling that they 'belong' in the family that is church.

Links

- Statistics come from Contact a Family: www.cafamily.org.uk/professionals/research. This is a great organisation whose website is a mine of valuable information.
- Children Matter has many helpful articles about children with additional needs. Visit their website and register for a free weekly e-newsletter: www.childrenmatter.net
- Children Worldwide: www.childrenworldwide.co.uk. You can contact the author of this chapter via this website, which contains lots of useful information.

'Walk with me'

I'm walking for a thousand people who cannot walk
I'm talking for a thousand people who cannot talk
Let their voices be heard
Let their stories be told
I'm looking for a thousand people to walk with me.

Milford-on-Sea, 8 March 2009, 9.30am. It was cold! The temperature was a few degrees above zero but the wind, close to gale force, made it feel much colder. I had come prepared but, even with every layer of clothing on and waterproofs on top, I was shivering.

Four days earlier I'd set off from Westminster in central London on an extraordinary journey. The 'Walk with me' campaign, a thousand-mile walk divided into ten weeks of 100 miles each, was spread over eight months of 2009. Twenty miles a day for five days is quite demanding; the route since leaving London had taken me via Dorking, Worthing, Winchester and Southampton to meet up with people from church-based groups in partnership with Prospects and others supported by Prospects at home. The idea was to have people walking with me every day for some or all of the route.

Pete and Ozzie were my companions for the first four miles from Milford that day, but from Barton-on-Sea I was on my own. The wind was getting stronger, picking up sand and blasting it into my face, the wind doing its best to make me stumble by blowing my legs this way and that. It was a struggle even to step forward, and I was beginning to feel sorry for myself.

I had known, of course, that it would be hard going. It was 20 years at least since I'd walked 20 miles in a day, let alone doing it for five consecutive days. Walking the streets of London out to Dorking had given me blisters on one foot; the cross-country route to Worthing the next day put blisters on the other. I couldn't work out which foot to favour as I limped along.

'You think you're struggling?' It was almost as though spoken aloud, so clear was the voice, but there was no one else around. 'This is what it's like,' the voice went on, 'for people with learning disabilities and their families day after day, month after month, year in, year out. They struggle to get education for their sons and daughters; they struggle for enough money to meet their families' needs; they struggle for acceptance in society and often in the church too.'

I was pretty clear, I thought, about my campaign aims. Walk a thousand miles, get a thousand people to walk with me and get sponsored, raise £100,000 and speak in lots of churches.

I began to realise what God was saying. Laudable though my campaign aims were, God's agenda was much wider, more comprehensive. There were matters of social injustice about which God was passionate. He began speaking to me about them.

I'm crying for a thousand people who never lived
I'm grieving for a thousand people who've been bereaved
God forgive what we've done
In the name of Jesus your Son
I'm looking for a thousand people to weep with me.

I never intended to write a campaign song. What happened next shocked me for two reasons—first, because it's not how songs are usually written, and second, because God broke my heart for the things that break his. As I walked, God began showing me issues that he's passionate about, and gave me my mind. How would I ever remember it all? Pete was waiting for me at the harbour: 'What on earth has happened to you?'

I sat on the ground, leaning against a wall, and scribbled out the song with a stub of pencil. It was etched on my brain. I sang it that evening for the first time and then at almost every gathering over the remaining nine weeks of the walk. It became the campaign song, but of one thing I am certain: I didn't write it. Yes, it was my stub of pencil, my voice singing the words, but I believe the song was from God—a message he wanted me to share and a message he wants his people and his church to respond to.

'Walk with me' has been recorded on the Daybreak label (© 2012), and you can listen to the song and download an MP3 version from this website:

www.prospects.org.uk/walkwithmemp3

Appendix
Including people with learning disabilities: Accessible teaching

Hope for ever

This is a narrative story teaching about heaven (written in the first person, as if told by John).

Hi! My name's John. You've probably heard of me. I'm one of Jesus' special friends—one of the twelve disciples. We spent three years with Jesus learning from him. It was wonderful to see Jesus healing people, turning water into wine, feeding 5000 people with a little boy's picnic lunch. And the things he used to talk about! He taught us about God and his kingdom, he taught us about prayer, and Jesus taught us about heaven, too. That's what I want to tell you about today.

When I think about the time we spent with Jesus, I have to think back a long way. You see, I'm an old man now. I've spent many years being a follower of Jesus. After Jesus was killed and raised from the dead, we worked very hard to start the Christian church, to tell people about Jesus and to encourage them to be strong Christians. It all went well for a while, but some people didn't like us talking about Jesus—they tried to stop us.

Well, to cut a long story short, what happened to me is that soldiers came to arrest me one day. They took me away from home and put me on a ship that brought me to a prison on an island. So I'm a prisoner now. I spend lots of time on my own, but I don't mind that because I can spend time worshipping Jesus. I spend hours in prayer, singing praise and worship songs and remembering what Jesus told us. One day when I was worshipping, I had an amazing vision—like a dream. God showed me what heaven is like. It's that vision of heaven that I want to share with you now.

Heaven is a place of worship. Right in the middle of everything is Jesus, and the whole of heaven is worshipping Jesus all the time. Heaven is filled with the sound of praise: 'Holy, Holy, Holy is the Lord God Almighty.' There are angels worshipping Jesus— thousands, millions of angels, all singing, 'Jesus is worthy to receive honour, glory and praise.'

And there were people there too. Every person who believes and trusts in Jesus goes to heaven. So every Christian who has died is already there. Thousands, millions of people, all worshipping Jesus. People from every country on earth, together in heaven because they are followers of Jesus.

As I looked around heaven, do you know what I noticed? Nobody was sick—there were no illnesses. Nobody was in pain; nobody was crying. Nobody was in a wheelchair or using crutches. I was so excited about heaven, I just had to write it all down. You will find it in the book of Revelation, in the Bible.

Heaven is really good news for people with disabilities. In heaven you won't need a walking frame or wheelchair. You'll be able to jump and dance. We won't need glasses or hearing aids— our bodies will work properly. You won't need to worry about not being understood. Everyone will know what you mean. There will be no sadness, no pain, and no more dying.

But the best thing about heaven is Jesus. It's always good to worship Jesus when we meet in our churches or special groups. How much better it will be when we worship Jesus in heaven! He *will be right there with us, so we'll be able to tell him how much we love him. Won't that be fantastic? One thing you can look forward to about heaven—we will be with the Lord for ever and ever and ever.*

Application that could follow John's story

Everything we heard from John, and everything we read in the Bible, tells us that heaven is a wonderful place. It's something to look forward to, and if you are a believer, a follower of Jesus, you will get there one day. But there's one thing that some people worry about. They like the idea of heaven, but people die before they go there. It's the idea of dying they don't like. So let's think about what happens when we die.

First of all, it's nothing to be frightened about. Everybody will die one day. You might be ill first. It will be like going to sleep at any other time. The difference will be when you wake up. It won't be your alarm clock, mum or dad, carer or friend that wakes you. It will be Jesus. He'll take you to the special place he's got ready for you. There will be crowds of people waiting to welcome you. It will be better than the best party you've ever been to. And the party will go on for ever!

Do you remember, earlier on, we were hearing about some things you won't find in heaven? No pain or suffering, no crying or tears, no trouble with speaking or understanding. There are quite a few things that give us problems now that we won't have in heaven. On the cards being passed round, you'll find a list of things. I wonder which of them you'll be most glad to get rid of—to be without. Have a look at the card and talk with the people around you. Tick any that are a problem for you now.

Tony Phelps-Jones has spent 25 years experimenting with how to make Christian worship and Bible teaching more accessible and relevant for people with learning disabilities. As a musician and songwriter, he began developing a style of worship that made it possible for people to join in regardless of reading, memory or vocal skills. His songs are characterised by the use of everyday language, repetition and a technique he calls 'echo songs' in which the leader sings a line and the congregation listens, then copies and sings the same line back.

Tony is passionate not only about inclusive worship but also about sharing the good news of Jesus clearly and simply so that people with learning disabilities can understand and respond. He is continuing the work started by Prospects founders David and Madeleine Potter, and proof of the effectiveness of the ministry is that over 200 churches now partner with Prospects to run a discipleship group for adults with learning disabilities.

Tony is a respected speaker and trainer and has led ministry teams at many major conferences, advising them on how to become more inclusive and helping to change the Christian public's attitudes towards disabled people.

Among the resources he has developed are five CDs of worship songs, two of which have been made into DVDs with Makaton signing to the songs, and a series of twelve books of accessible daily Bible reading notes, all of which are available on CDs in audio format.

He lives in Hampshire, is married to Tua and has two grown-up sons. He likes to keep fit by running, playing squash and hill-walking. Tony's father had polio as a young man and walked with sticks, unable to run around like other dads, so Tony grew up with disability but never thought of his father as disabled. Undoubtedly, a childhood in which disability felt normal prepared him for the career he has followed.

Enjoyed

this book?

Write a review—we'd love to hear what you think.
Email: reviews@brf.org.uk

Keep up to date—receive details of our new books as they happen.
Sign up for email news and select your interest groups at:
www.brfonline.org.uk/findoutmore/

Follow us on Twitter @brfonline

By post—to receive new title information by post (UK only), complete the form below and post to: BRF Mailing Lists, 15 The Chambers, Vineyard, Abingdon, Oxfordshire, OX14 3FE

Your Details
Name _____
Address_____
_____
Town/City _____ Post Code _____
Email_____

Your Interest Groups (*Please tick as appropriate)	
☐ Advent/Lent	☐ Messy Church
☐ Bible Reading & Study	☐ Pastoral
☐ Children's Books	☐ Prayer & Spirituality
☐ Discipleship	☐ Resources for Children's Church
☐ Leadership	☐ Resources for Schools

Support your local bookshop
Ask about their new title information schemes.